Fresh Bread & Bakes
FROM YOUR
BREAD MACHINE

Discover how bread and cakes should taste
with these easy-to-use recipes

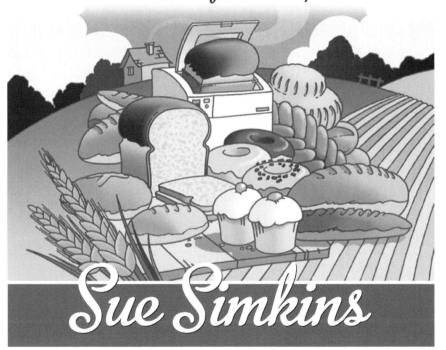

Sue Simkins

Spring Hill

For David, David and Edie

Published by Spring Hill, an imprint of How To Books Ltd.
Spring Hill House, Spring Hill Road
Begbroke, Oxford OX5 1RX
United Kingdom
Tel: (01865) 375794
Fax: (01865) 379162
info@howtobooks.co.uk
www.howtobooks.co.uk

First published 2011

How To Books greatly reduce the carbon footprint of their books by sourcing their typesetting and printing in the UK.

British Library Cataloguing in Publication Data
A catalogue record for this book is available from the British Library

ISBN: 978 1 905862 71 9

Cover design by Baseline Arts Ltd, Oxford
Produced for How To Books by Deer Park Productions, Tavistock, Devon
Typeset by PDQ Typesetting Ltd, Newcastle-under-Lyme, Staffordshire
Printed and bound in Great Britain by MPG Books Group, Bodmin, Cornwall

Fresh Bread & Bakes
FROM YOUR
BREAD MACHINE

Contents

3   Sweet Loaves, Buns and Tea Breads   110

4 Easy Cakes From Your Bread Machine   156

Acknowledgements

Thank you to my family and friends and to everyone who helped with the making of this book.

As ever, thank you to Fanny Charles and everyone at the *Blackmore Vale Magazine*.

Very special thanks to: Moira Blake of Dorset Pastry for all her help and encouragement and specialist knowledge; home economist Fiona Grierson of recipes2share.com, for her rigorous and professional recipe testing, especially in the cake section, and for generously sharing her inspiring ideas; professional baker of many years' standing Frank Dike, for unstintingly sharing a lifetime's experience of baking.

And, finally, a huge thank you to everyone at How To Books.

Thank you all very much indeed.

Introduction

'Give us this day our daily bread…'

People have made and eaten bread since the first farmers learnt to grow and harvest grain way back in prehistory. Bread is a staple food and the word itself has come to mean food and nourishment in general. Apart from those unable to eat wheat for health reasons, most people respond instantly and automatically to the sight and smell of freshly baked bread and you probably won't come across many people in your life who don't love toast.

Of all the home-baked goodies you can make for your friends and family, few are as enthusiastically appreciated as freshly baked bread. A bread machine can help you bake your own bread simply and easily.

MACHINES BEHAVING DIFFERENTLY

Bread machine makes and models can vary quite considerably in performance and it's helpful to know what you are taking on.

Some machines have a more efficient mixing action than others. Not to get too technical, the more vigorously the machine mixes, the more the starch in the flour is broken up and the more liquid can be absorbed. This means that machines with a more efficient action use a greater proportion of liquid to flour – and produce a more voluminous loaf with a better crumb structure, a fresher, more enticing smell and better keeping qualities. In the case of white bread, the colour may also be brighter.

Equally, when you are making bread by hand, kneading is a crucial part of the process and one person may have a better technique and more strength than another. The person who is more thorough and adept at kneading will be able to produce a better loaf than the one who is not quite so skilled.

Again, something similar happens with bread machines. Some machines have more efficient, stronger kneading actions than others and make excellent, fine-textured, flavoursome bread.

When you are baking bread, the ingredients work best at slightly warm temperatures, and not so well when cold. Some machines have very efficient sensors and are capable of bringing the ingredients up to the ideal temperature before mixing starts and are better insulated against outside temperatures should the room they are in be too cold or too draughty – or, conversely, too hot and humid.

If you possibly can, aim to buy one of the more efficient models, which admittedly are more expensive. They are easier to use and in the long run more economical on flour than some of the more competitively priced models. Anyone who has ever looked at reviews of bread machines will have noticed a couple of brands – and one brand in particular – always score well and there is no doubt that these are excellent machines that will give you many years of faithful service.

However, with a little understanding and coaxing, all machines can make a tasty loaf.

THE GLUTEN FACTOR

Another helpful aspect of bread making to understand is the importance of gluten and how it behaves.

Gluten comes from plant protein, which is found in wheat and to a lesser extent in similar grass-type grains such as barley, rye and oats.

In very, very general terms, gluten acts as a kind of stretchy casing that holds in the carbon dioxide that the fermentation of the yeast produces. This helps the bread to rise well and also contributes to the familiar and characteristic slightly resistant, chewy texture of bread.

Are protein and gluten the same?

Very simply, when you buy strong bread flour, you are buying flour that is high in protein. 'Hard' or 'strong' flour is flour that is high in protein while 'soft' or 'weak' flour is lower in protein. Gluten is developed *from* protein. When you add water this enables the gluten to be activated, so the higher a flour is in protein the more gluten it will potentially be able to create.

Plain water makes a strong mix with long, stretchy gluten strands – known as a 'long' dough. Once fat enters the equation the gluten strands can't stretch as far and a softer, 'shorter' dough is produced. This is because when you add fat to flour, the fat envelopes the gluten and the water cannot penetrate and activate it: in fact it retards the gluten development. This is why adding milk makes a 'shorter', more tender dough than water because milk contains fat.

Heat also activates gluten and plenty of kneading and working of the dough produces friction, which also generates heat.

Building up the gluten

Gluten potential is present in strong bread flour but needs to be worked on and helped to develop.

When you add water to flour, the proteins in the flour bind with the water and are able to bind with each other to form a stretchy bundle of gluten molecules. The more you work the dough, the more gluten develops as more proteins bind with other proteins and water. This is one reason why a generous proportion of water to flour is a good thing – it aids good gluten development.

While the dough is being kneaded, the yeast is also hard at work releasing more and more bubbles of air which are encased by the ever-developing stretchy gluten 'casing' like a honeycomb of bubbles.

Incidentally, flour with a high protein content is usually produced at high altitudes in cold temperatures. This is why winter wheat is grown: cold temperatures maximise the protein potential, therefore winter wheat, which is sown in September and in the ground over the winter, contains more protein than spring-sown wheat. With regard to altitude, there are no high mountain ranges in Britain, therefore Britain cannot produce very high-protein flour but over-wintered wheat is higher in protein than that sown in spring. Having said this, Canadian spring-sown wheat is likely to be higher in protein than British winter wheat. The best high-protein flour comes from Canada, Italy, the French Alps and parts of Eastern Europe with high altitudes and cold, harsh winters.

Since weather conditions influence the protein content of wheat, inevitably wheat – and flour – quality varies from year to year and region to region. Always buy good-quality strong bread flour for your bread making but be prepared for there to be a slight amount of variation in performance from year to year.

WATER AND SALT

Water

Ideally, bread dough is approximately 40% water: too much water and the loaf will stay small and flat, the texture will look too open and feel too damp and dense; too little water and the loaf will still be too small and compacted and the texture will be too dry. In a white loaf the colour may look a bit dull and grey. Warm water works best for bread dough. Dough can also be affected by the hardness or softness of the water – but we won't go into that just now!

Salt

All we need to know at this point is: salt adds flavour, slows down fermentation and strengthens the gluten: we won't get more complicated than that!

Sugar and fat

Bread has four basic ingredients: flour, water, salt and yeast. Any other ingredient is an *improver*, not an essential. Sugar will help fermentation, fat will soften the crumb and both will add flavour but, except in the case of a brioche-type dough, you don't need too much of either.

YOUR MACHINE'S INSTRUCTION BOOK

This book isn't meant to replace your instruction book but to work alongside it and complement it.

You will always need your own machine's instruction booklet: as mentioned earlier, different makes and models of machines vary and there will always be times when you need to refer back to your machine's own specific instructions. If you have lost your instruction book, it's worth asking the manufacturers to send you another.

CHOICE OF INGREDIENTS

Flour

Unless otherwise stated, use strong white and strong wholemeal bread flours.

Yeast
Use quick yeast made for use in bread machines.

Salt
Finely crushed or ground sea salt, particularly Maldon salt, works well but use ordinary table salt if you prefer. You must use actual salt as salt substitutes won't react properly with the yeast.

Oil
Unless otherwise stated, use some kind of mild oil that doesn't impart a specific taste: rapeseed, sunflower and mild olive are all good.

Butter
Use pure butter and not a spread containing vegetable fat. Salted or unsalted are both suitable.

Sugar
Unless otherwise stated, use granulated sugar. Unrefined is good but white is fine.

Eggs
Unless otherwise stated, use medium-size eggs.

TAKING CARE OF THE BREAD PAN

Never ease a loaf out with a knife or anything metal or you will damage the inside of your bread pan. Leave the loaf to cool for a couple of minutes before you turn it out: it will begin to shrink away from the sides as it cools. If something does get stuck, use a robust plastic picnic knife to ease it out.

Sometimes the mixing blade can get stuck in the loaf. Once the loaf is cool it's easy to get it out with your fingers; again, don't use anything metal as you will scratch the blade.

Incidentally, if you leave the loaf in the machine for too long once it is ready, it will become damp and wrinkly. It will still be edible but not quite as nice.

STORING BREAD

It's also worth getting yourself a large plastic sandwich box style bread bin as it's an efficient way to keep your bread fresh for longer.

Once home-made bread is a day or so old, it makes the most fantastic toast.

OVEN TEMPERATURE CONVERSIONS

Mark 1	275°F	140°C
Mark 2	300°F	150°C
Mark 3	325°F	170°C
Mark 4	350°F	180°C
Mark 5	375°F	190°C
Mark 6	400°F	200°C
Mark 7	425°F	220°C
Mark 8	450°F	230°C

OVEN TEMPERATURES

Please be aware that individual oven performance varies tremendously.

Some ovens will happily bake bread at 180°C (fan ovens) but it is more usual to bake bread at 200-220°C (fan ovens) or equivalent. For this reason, baking temperatures are given as 180-220°C or equivalent. Practice will tell which is correct for your oven. Keep notes so you know what you are doing.

USEFUL-SIZED BAKING TINS

Here are the most useful sizes of baking tins you can use to bake loaves and rolls in the oven with dough made in the machine. Heavier, better-quality baking tins conduct heat more efficiently than anything thin and flimsy and have a longer life.

Large baking tray, ideally x 2
A baking tray that just fits comfortably inside your oven.

12-cup muffin tin, ideally x 2
This is useful for buns and rolls.

12-cup mini-muffin tin x 2

Loose-bottomed cake tins
It's handy to have the following sizes for some sweet breads, rounds and batches of rolls and buns, pizzas and baguettes:

18cm cake tin
23cm cake tin

20cm brownie tin
Pizza trays x 2
Baguette tray x 2

Mini-loaf tins
Usually sold in packs of four, these are brilliant for sweet, dinky mini-loaf rolls. It's useful to have 12 if possible.

1
Loaves Made Entirely in the Machine

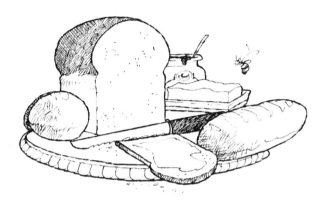

Your bread machine will bake whole loaves for you from beginning to end, which is particularly helpful during a busy working week.

PROGRAMMES

Your machine will have a selection of different programmes, usually including:

- a **Basic White** programme which is useful for the majority of loaves you will make with white flour or white flour with a percentage of other flours added;

- a **Raisin** option which is useful for when you are adding dried fruit and so on where the pieces are to remain whole rather than broken up and incorporated into the mixture;

- a **French Bake** programme, which is extra long and allows the dough more time to develop, giving a more open texture and yeasty flavour. The baking temperature may also be a little hotter and the crust crispier;

◆ a **Whole wheat** programme which is also longer and allows the gluten more time to develop. It may also spend more time at the beginning of the cycle gently warming the ingredients to help with gluten development.

ORDER OF INGREDIENTS

When adding the ingredients to the bread pan, the most important aspect to bear in mind is to keep the yeast dry and away from the salt and sugar in the very first stages.

The preferred method for adding ingredients is usually to put the liquid in first; the salt and the sugar, spaced apart; then the flour; and the yeast on top, last of all. This works well with most machines and is particularly helpful with some machines that have a less vigorous action and struggle slightly to gather up all the flour into the dough ball at the beginning of the kneading cycle.

If in doubt, add the ingredients in the precise order specified by your instruction book.

FLOUR TO LIQUID RATIOS

An alternative amount of flour and liquid is suggested for some recipes. The second amount may be better suited to the more competitively priced makes of bread machine, which tend to use a greater proportion of flour to liquid.

Mixtures containing significant quantities of moist fruit or vegetable such as apple, banana and so on, tend to perform successfully in most types of machine without altering the original amounts of flour and liquid in the mixture. The final amount of dough may be slightly smaller in volume when made in the more competitively priced machines.

Richer, brioche-type mixtures containing generous quantities of butter and egg also tend to perform successfully in most types of machine without altering the original amounts of flour and liquid in the mixture. Again, the final amount of dough may be slightly smaller in volume when made in the more competitively priced machines.

Always use the measuring spoon that comes with your bread machine for both dry and liquid ingredients; and always fill the spoons to the top and level off dry ingredients.

Check with your machine's instruction booklet recipes to see the typical flour to liquid ratio for your machine.

You may also need to give the machine a helping hand to incorporate all the flour at the beginning: use a flexible spatula to scrape the loose flour from the sides of the bread pan.

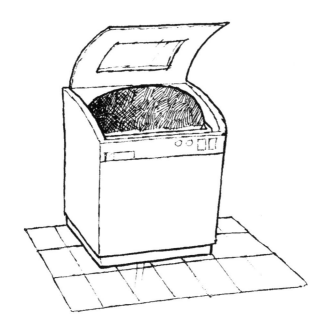

Basic White Loaf

This is a basic, everyday loaf and is the one you will probably make most often when making a loaf entirely in the machine. In addition to the basic four ingredients of flour, yeast, water and salt, the loaf contains sugar to help the yeast do its work and oil to soften the crumb and help with the keeping qualities.

300ml warm water   1 tablespoon sugar
2 tablespoons mild oil   400g strong white bread flour
1 teaspoon salt   1 teaspoon yeast

1. Pour the water and oil into the bread pan of your machine and add the salt and sugar, placing them at different ends of the pan.

2. Add the flour and put the yeast centrally on the top.

3. Fix the bread pan into position, making sure it is settled securely. Set the machine to the **Basic White** programme with **Medium** loaf size and **Light** crust setting. Press Start.

4. Once the loaf is ready, take the bread pan out of the machine and leave the loaf to settle for just a few moments: this will give it time to contract slightly away from the sides of the pan.

5. Then slide it out, on its side, onto a wooden board. Pick it up and stand it upright on a cooling rack.

6. Once it is completely cold, store it in an airtight plastic box or a sealed plastic bag.

If the flour to liquid ratio doesn't seem quite right for your machine, in that the amount of liquid seems too great, try increasing the flour measurement to 500g and decrease the water to 260ml. Check with your machine's instruction booklet recipes to see the typical flour to liquid ratio for your machine.

You may also need to give the machine a helping hand to incorporate all the flour at the beginning: use a flexible spatula to scrape the loose flour from the sides of the bread pan.

Basic Loaf with Wholemeal

This is a slight variation on the basic white loaf with added wholemeal for flavour and goodness.

300ml warm water

2 tablespoons mild oil

1 teaspoon salt

1 tablespoon sugar

300g strong white bread flour

100g strong wholemeal bread flour

1 teaspoon yeast

1. Pour the water and oil into the bread pan of your machine and add the salt and sugar, placing them at different ends of the pan.

2. Add the flours and put the yeast centrally on the top.

3. Fix the bread pan into position, making sure it is settled securely. Select the **Basic White** programme with **Medium** loaf size and **Light** crust setting. Press start.

4. Once the loaf is ready, take the bread pan out of the machine and leave the loaf to settle for just a few moments: this will give it time to contract slightly away from the sides of the pan

5. Then slide it out, on its side, onto a wooden board. Pick it up and stand it upright on a cooling rack.

If the flour to liquid ratio doesn't seem quite right for your machine, in that the amount of liquid seems too great, try increasing the total flour measurement to 500g and decrease the water to 260ml. Check with your machine's instruction booklet recipes to see the typical flour to liquid ratio for your machine.

Basic Loaf with Malted Granary Flour

This is another delicious variation on the basic white loaf with added malted grain flour for a malty flavour and extra texture.

300ml warm water	300g strong white bread flour
2 tablespoons mild oil	100g strong malted multigrain bread flour
1 teaspoon salt	1 teaspoon yeast
1 tablespoon sugar	

1. Pour the water and oil into the bread pan of your machine and add the salt and sugar, placing them at different ends of the pan.

2. Add the flours and put the yeast centrally on the top.

3. Fix the bread pan into position, making sure it is settled securely. Select the **Basic White** programme with **Medium** loaf size and **Light** crust setting. Press Start.

4. Once the loaf is ready, take the bread pan out of the machine and leave the loaf to settle for just a few moments: this will give it time to contract slightly away from the sides of the pan.

5. Then slide it out, on its side, onto a wooden board. Pick it up and stand it upright on a cooling rack.

If the flour to liquid ratio doesn't seem quite right for your machine, in that the amount of liquid seems too great, try increasing the total flour measurement to 500g and decrease the water to 260ml. Check with your machine's instruction booklet recipes to see the typical flour to liquid ratio for your machine.

Basic Loaf with Mixed Seeds and Grains

This is the basic white loaf with malty goodness and extra grains for more flavour and more texture.

300ml warm water

2 tablespoons mild oil

1 teaspoon salt

1 tablespoon sugar

300g strong white bread flour

100g strong malted multigrain bread flour

1 teaspoon yeast

150g mixed seeds, such as sunflower, pumpkin, linseed and hemp

1. Pour the water and oil into the bread pan of your machine and add the salt and sugar, placing them at different ends of the pan.

2. Add the flours and put the yeast centrally on the top.

3. Fix the bread pan into position, making sure it is settled securely. Set the machine to the **Basic White** programme with **Raisin** option with **Medium** loaf size and **Light** crust setting.

4. Either put the seeds into the raisin compartment, if your machine has one, or set the raisin beep and add them when it sounds. Press Start.

5. Once the loaf is ready, take the bread pan out of the machine and leave the loaf to settle for just a few moments: this will give it time to contract slightly away from the sides of the pan.

6. Then slide it out, on its side, onto a wooden board. Pick it up and stand it upright on a cooling rack.

If the flour to liquid ratio doesn't seem quite right for your machine, in that the amount of liquid seems too great, try increasing the total flour measurement to 500g and decrease the water to 260ml. Check with your machine's instruction booklet recipes to see the typical flour to liquid ratio for your machine.

ADDING OTHER FLOURS TO THE MAIN RECIPE

Once you have got the hang of these variations on the **Basic White Loaf**, you might like to try experimenting with adding other types of flour. You could replace 75–100g of white flour with spelt flour or buckwheat or rye. Barleycorn mix is also good. Alternatively, try kamut flour. Like spelt flour, this is another ancient wheat-type grain: it is particularly high in selenium, which many modern diets can lack, and has a lovely sweet taste.

Half and Half Basic White and Hovis Loaf

This makes a fine-textured brown loaf.

300ml warm water	200g strong white bread flour
2 tablespoons mild oil	200g Hovis strong wholemeal bread flour
1 teaspoon salt	1 teaspoon quick yeast
1 tablespoon sugar	

1. Pour the water and oil into the bread pan of your machine and add the salt and sugar, placing them at different ends of the pan.

2. Add the flours and put the yeast centrally on the top.

3. Fix the bread pan into position, making sure it is settled securely. Select the **Basic White** programme with **Medium** loaf size and **Light** crust setting. Press Start.

4. Once the loaf is ready, take the bread pan out of the machine and leave the loaf to settle for just a few moments: this will give it time to contract slightly away from the sides of the pan.

5. Then slide it out, on its side, onto a wooden board. Pick it up and stand it upright on a cooling rack.

If the flour to liquid ratio doesn't seem quite right for your machine, in that the amount of liquid seems too great, try increasing the total flour measurement to 500g and decrease the water to 260ml. Check with your machine's instruction booklet recipes to see the typical flour to liquid ratio for your machine.

Basic Loaf with Oatbran

The oatbran gives the basic loaf an extra sweetness and texture, as well as some useful fibre.

300ml warm water
2 tablespoons mild oil
1 teaspoon salt
1 tablespoon sugar

300g strong white bread flour
100g oatbran
1 teaspoon yeast

1. Pour the water and oil into the bread pan of your machine and add the salt and sugar, placing them at different ends of the pan.

2. Add the flour and oatbran and put the yeast centrally on the top.

3. Fix the bread pan into position, making sure it is settled securely. Select the **Basic White** programme with **Medium** loaf size and **Light** crust setting. Press Start.

4. Once the loaf is ready, take the bread pan out of the machine and leave the loaf to settle for just a few moments: this will give it time to contract slightly away from the sides of the pan.

5. Then slide it out, on its side, onto a wooden board. Pick it up and stand it upright on a cooling rack.

If the flour to liquid ratio doesn't seem quite right for your machine, in that the amount of liquid seems too great, try increasing the flour measurement to 500g and decrease the water to 260ml. Check with your machine's instruction booklet recipes to see the typical flour to liquid ratio for your machine.

Basic Loaf with Cornmeal

This pale creamy yellow loaf makes an interesting change from the basic white.

You could use polenta but the texture will be quite different and discernibly 'bitty'. Polenta is cornmeal but more coarsely ground – giving more of a characteristic grittiness than the finer cornmeal.

....

300ml warm water

2 tablespoons mild oil

1 teaspoon salt

1 tablespoon sugar

300g strong white bread flour

100g finely ground cornmeal

1 teaspoon yeast

....

1. Pour the water and oil into the bread pan of your machine and add the salt and sugar, placing them at different ends of the pan.

2. Add the flour and cornmeal and put the yeast centrally on the top.

3. Fix the bread pan into position, making sure it is settled securely. Select the **Basic White** programme with **Medium** loaf size and **Light** crust setting. Press Start.

4. Once the loaf is ready, take the bread pan out of the machine and leave the loaf to settle for just a few moments: this will give it time to contract slightly away from the sides of the pan.

5. Then slide it out, on its side, onto a wooden board. Pick it up and stand it upright on a cooling rack.

If the flour to liquid ratio doesn't seem quite right for your machine, in that the amount of liquid seems too great, try increasing the flour measurement to 500g and decrease the water to 260ml. Check with your machine's instruction booklet recipes to see the typical flour to liquid ratio for your machine.

Basic Loaf with Potato

This loaf contains a relatively small amount of potato, but enough to make a difference. The finished loaf is fluffy and moist: it's beautiful eaten fresh with butter and it makes great toast the following day.

100g cold cooked potatoes, mashed or boiled
150ml warm water, use potato cooking water, if available
2 tablespoons mild oil

1 teaspoon salt
1 tablespoon sugar
400g strong white bread flour
1 teaspoon yeast

1. If the potatoes are not already mashed, mash them with a fork.

2. Pour the water and oil into the bread pan of your machine and add the potatoes. Place the salt and sugar at different ends of the pan.

3. Add the flour and put the yeast centrally on the top.

4. Fix the bread pan into position, making sure it is settled securely. Select the **Basic White** programme with **Medium** loaf size and **Light** crust setting. Press Start.

5. Once the loaf is ready, take the bread pan out of the machine and leave the loaf to settle for just a few moments: this will give it time to contract slightly away from the sides of the pan.

6. Then slide it out, on its side, onto a wooden board. Pick it up and stand it upright on a cooling rack.

Note: If you are using leftover potato mashed with vast amounts of butter and cream the bread may turn out a little on the heavy side.

This recipe is suitable for most types of bread machine.

Basic Loaf with Rice

This isn't unlike potato bread in texture as the extra starch in the rice gives the same light fluffiness. It works best with well-cooked rice; if you like your rice too 'al dente' it will tend to stay in separate grains and not be incorporated into the dough so well. Plus, the rice needs to contain a certain amount of moisture to enhance the bread.

260ml water	1 tablespoon sugar
1 tablespoon mild oil	400g strong white bread flour
100g cold boiled rice	1 teaspoon quick yeast
1 teaspoon salt	

1. Pour the water and oil into the bread pan of your machine and add the rice. Place the salt and sugar at different ends of the pan.

2. Add the flour and put the yeast centrally on the top.

3. Fix the bread pan into position, making sure it is settled securely. Select the **Basic White** programme with **Medium** loaf size and **Light** crust setting. Press Start.

4. Once the loaf is ready, take the bread pan out of the machine and leave the loaf to settle for just a few moments: this will give it time to contract slightly away from the sides of the pan.

5. Then slide it out, on its side, onto a wooden board. Pick it up and stand it upright on a cooling rack.

This recipe is suitable for most types of bread machine. If the finished loaf seems a fraction too moist, try decreasing the water by 10ml the next time.

Basic Loaf with Courgette

The courgette gives an extra lightness and moisture to this unusual loaf and you will notice it rises higher than normal. Courgette also imparts a subtle sweet flavour and extends the loaf's keeping qualities. If you look closely at the cut surface, you will notice small intriguing green flecks but you won't be able to actually taste courgette.

If seeds have begun to form, cut the courgettes lengthways and use a teaspoon to scrape out the seedy bits.

160ml warm water	1 tablespoon sugar
2 tablespoons mild oil	400g strong white bread flour
100g courgette, peeled and grated	1 teaspoon quick yeast
1 teaspoon salt	

1. Pour the water and oil into the bread pan of your machine and add the courgette. Place the salt and sugar at different ends of the pan.

2. Add the flour and put the yeast centrally on the top.

3. Fix the bread pan into position, making sure it is settled securely. Select the **Basic White** programme with **Medium** loaf size and **Light** crust setting. Press Start.

4. Once the loaf is ready, take the bread pan out of the machine and leave the loaf to settle for just a few moments: this will give it time to contract slightly away from the sides of the pan.

5. Then slide it out, on its side, onto a wooden board. Pick it up and stand it upright on a cooling rack.

This recipe is suitable for most types of bread machine.

Basic Loaf with Bran and Raisin

This is a lovely easy fruit loaf with a bit of extra fibre.

320ml warm water	400g strong white bread flour
2 tablespoons mild oil	50g wheat bran
1 teaspoon salt	1 teaspoon yeast
1 tablespoon runny honey	150g raisins

1. Pour the water and oil into the bread pan of your machine and add the salt and honey, placing them at different ends of the pan.

2. Add the flour and bran and put the yeast centrally on the top.

3. Fix the bread pan into position, making sure it is settled securely. Set the machine to the **Basic White** programme with **Raisin** option with **Medium** loaf size and **Light** crust setting.

4. Either put the raisins into the raisin compartment, if your machine has one, or set the raisin beep and add them when it sounds. Press Start.

5. Once the loaf is ready, take the bread pan out of the machine and leave the loaf to settle for just a few moments: this will give it time to contract slightly away from the sides of the pan.

6. Then slide it out, on its side, onto a wooden board. Pick it up and stand it upright on a cooling rack.

If the flour to liquid ratio doesn't seem quite right for your machine, in that the amount of liquid seems too great, try increasing the flour measurement to 460g.

You may also need to give the machine a helping hand to incorporate all the flour at the beginning: use a flexible spatula to scrape the loose flour from the sides of the bread pan.

Milk Loaf

This loaf has a lovely extra soft and fine texture. Skimmed milk works best but you could also use semi-skimmed. Milk loaves keep well but they are at their softest and most delicious when fresh.

300ml warm skimmed milk

2 tablespoons mild oil

1 teaspoon salt

1 tablespoon sugar

400g strong white bread flour

1 teaspoon quick yeast

1. Pour the milk and oil into the bread pan of your machine and add the salt and sugar, placing them at different ends of the pan.

2. Add the flour and put the yeast centrally on the top.

3. Fix the bread pan into position, making sure it is settled securely. Select the **Basic White** programme with **Medium** loaf size and **Light** crust setting. Press Start.

4. Once the loaf is ready, take the bread pan out of the machine and leave the loaf to settle for just a few moments: this will give it time to contract slightly away from the sides of the pan.

5. Then slide it out, on its side, onto a wooden board. Pick it up and stand it upright on a cooling rack.

If the flour to liquid ratio doesn't seem quite right for your machine, in that the amount of liquid seems too great, try increasing the flour measurement to 500g and decrease the milk to 260ml. Check with your machine's instruction booklet recipes to see the typical flour to liquid ratio for your machine.

Plain and Simple Basic Loaf

Here is a perfectly plain and simple, basic loaf. It contains just the four basic bread ingredients of flour and water, yeast and salt. It has a slightly rougher and readier feel to it than bread containing fat and sugar. It also makes very good toast. You may find it doesn't keep quite as well as a loaf containing some form of fat.

300ml warm water	400g strong white bread flour
1 teaspoon salt	1 teaspoon quick yeast

1. Pour the water into the bread pan of your machine and add the salt.

2. Add the flour and put the yeast centrally on the top.

3. Fix the bread pan into position, making sure it is settled securely. Select the **Basic White** programme with **Medium** loaf size and **Light** crust setting. Press Start.

4. Once the loaf is ready, take the bread pan out of the machine and leave the loaf to settle for just a few moments: this will give it time to contract slightly away from the sides of the pan.

5. Then slide it out, on its side, onto a wooden board. Pick it up and stand it upright on a cooling rack.

If the flour to liquid ratio doesn't seem quite right for your machine, in that the amount of liquid seems too great, try increasing the flour measurement to 500g and decrease the water to 260ml. Check with your machine's instruction booklet recipes to see the typical flour to liquid ratio for your machine.

Wholemeal Loaf

This has a beautiful sweet, nutty flavour. There is a little more water than usual in this recipe as wholemeal flour tends to absorb more liquid than white. The wholewheat programme of your machine is essential for best results.

320ml warm water   1 tablespoon sugar
2 tablespoons mild oil   400g strong wholemeal bread flour
1 teaspoon salt   1 teaspoon quick yeast

1. Pour the water and oil into the bread pan of your machine and add the salt and sugar, placing them at different ends of the pan.

2. Add the flour and put the yeast centrally on the top.

3. Fix the bread pan into position, making sure it is settled securely. Select the **Whole wheat** programme with **Medium** loaf size and **Light** crust setting. Press Start.

4. Once the loaf is ready, take the bread pan out of the machine and leave the loaf to settle for just a few moments: this will give it time to contract slightly away from the sides of the pan.

5. Then slide it out, on its side, onto a wooden board. Pick it up and stand it upright on a cooling rack.

If the flour to liquid ratio doesn't seem quite right for your machine, in that the amount of liquid seems too great, try increasing the flour measurement to 500g and decrease the water to 280ml. Check with your machine's instruction booklet recipes to see the typical flour to liquid ratio for your machine.

Fruit Bread

This is a simple and easy fruit bread that is delicious sliced and buttered: try it lightly toasted when it is a day or two old.

300ml recently brewed warm tea: Earl Grey works well	1 tablespoon caster sugar
	400g strong white bread flour
2 tablespoons mild oil	1 teaspoon yeast
1 teaspoon salt	150g mixed raisins, sultanas and currants

1. Pour the tea and oil into the bread pan of your machine and add the salt and sugar, placing them at different ends of the pan.

2. Add the flour and put the yeast centrally on the top.

3. Fix the bread pan into position, making sure it is settled securely. Set the machine to the **Basic White** programme with **Raisin** option with **Medium** loaf size and **Light** crust setting.

4. Either put the dried fruit into the raisin compartment, if your machine has one, or set the raisin beep and add them when it sounds. Press Start.

5. Once the loaf is ready, take the bread pan out of the machine and leave the loaf to settle for just a few moments: this will give it time to contract slightly away from the sides of the pan.

6. Then slide it out, on its side, onto a wooden board. Pick it up and stand it upright on a cooling rack.

If the flour to liquid ratio doesn't seem quite right for your machine, in that the amount of liquid seems too great, try increasing the flour measurement to 500g and decrease the tea to 260ml. Check with your machine's instruction booklet recipes to see the typical flour to liquid ratio for your machine.

Lavender and Honey Bread

You can also shape this unusual loaf yourself and bake it in the oven if you use the dough programme on your machine. See the chapter on Dough and, for Lavender and Honey Buns, the chapter on Sweet Dough.

A word of warning: be sure to use only the more common English lavender, *Lavandula angustifolia*, sometimes called *Lavendula officinalis* or *Lavandula spicata*. The tufty French lavender, *Lavandula stoechas*, can be toxic.

15–20 sprigs of lavender flowers still in bud	1 teaspoon salt
	1 tablespoon runny honey
300ml warm water	400g strong white bread flour
2 tablespoons mild oil	1 teaspoon quick yeast

1. Lay the lavender sprigs on kitchen paper for a while to dry out. Remove all the florets from the stalks and shake them lightly in a sieve.

2. Pour the water and oil into the bread pan of your machine and add the salt and honey, placing them at different ends of the pan. Put the flour on top and finally the yeast.

3. Fix the bread pan into position, making sure it is settled securely. Set the machine to the **Basic White** programme with **Raisin** option with **Medium** loaf size and **Light** crust setting.

4. Set the lavender aside for the raisin beep and add it then or put into the raisin dispenser if you have one. Press Start.

5. Once the loaf is ready, take the bread pan out of the machine and leave the loaf to settle for just a few moments: this will give it time to contract slightly away from the sides of the pan.

6. Then slide it out, on its side, onto a wooden board. Pick it up and stand it upright on a cooling rack.

If the flour to liquid ratio doesn't seem quite right for your machine, in that the amount of liquid seems too great, try increasing the flour measurement to 500g and decrease the water to 260ml. Check with your machine's instruction booklet recipes to see the typical flour to liquid ratio for your machine.

Apple Bread

The apple makes this loaf beautifully moist with a slight chewiness. It doesn't taste of apples as such but there is something elusive there in the background; it also helps the loaf to rise more and extends its keeping qualities. See Chapter 2, 'Dough Recipes', for more variations.

160ml warm water	1 tablespoon sugar
2 tablespoons mild oil	300g strong white bread flour
175g grated apple	100g strong wholemeal bread flour
1 teaspoon salt	1 teaspoon quick yeast

1. Pour the water and oil into the bread pan of your machine and add the apple. Place the salt and sugar at different ends of the pan.

2. Add the flours and put the yeast centrally on the top.

3. Fix the bread pan into position, making sure it is settled securely. Select the **Basic White** programme with **Medium** loaf size and **Light** crust setting. Press Start.

4. Once the loaf is ready, take the bread pan out of the machine and leave the loaf to settle for just a few moments: this will give it time to contract slightly away from the sides of the pan.

5. Then slide it out, on its side, onto a wooden board. Pick it up and stand it upright on a cooling rack.

This recipe is suitable for most types of bread machine.

Banana Bread

Banana bread isn't necessarily sweet as such. It's more that the banana adds a certain moistness and chewiness with a subtle flavour you can't quite put your finger on. See Chapter 2, 'Dough Recipes', for more variations.

160ml warm water

2 tablespoons mild oil

175g banana, peeled weight
(don't add more than this just
to 'use it up' or the bread will be
heavy)

1 teaspoon salt

1 tablespoon sugar

400g strong white bread flour

1 teaspoon quick yeast

1. Pour the water and oil into the bread pan of your machine and add the banana. Place the salt and sugar at different ends of the pan.

2. Add the flour and put the yeast centrally on the top.

3. Fix the bread pan into position, making sure it is settled securely. Select the **Basic White** programme with **Medium** loaf size and **Light** crust setting. Press Start.

4. Once the loaf is ready, take the bread pan out of the machine and leave the loaf to settle for just a few moments: this will give it time to contract slightly away from the sides of the pan.

5. Then slide it out, on its side, onto a wooden board. Pick it up and stand it upright on a cooling rack.

This recipe is suitable for most types of bread machine.

French-style Loaf

This is a tasty loaf to bake for a change. It has a good yeasty flavour, a slightly open, almost chewy texture and a crust that is crisp when first baked, becoming nicely chewy after a few hours. Try it for a Continental-style breakfast with butter and jam and milky coffee, or for lunch with cheeses or pâté.

As the programme is a long one, this loaf could be a good candidate for the timer option if you would like to enjoy it for breakfast. Check your own machine's instruction book for details on how to set the timer.

300ml water	400g strong white bread flour
1 teaspoon salt	1 teaspoon quick yeast
1 tablespoon sugar	

1. Pour the water into the bread pan of your machine and add the salt and sugar, placing them at different ends of the pan.

2. Add the flour and put the yeast centrally on the top.

3. Fix the bread pan into position, making sure it is settled securely. Set the machine to the **French bake** programme with **Medium** loaf size and **Light** crust setting. Press Start.

4. Once the loaf is ready, take the bread pan out of the machine and leave the loaf to settle for just a few moments: this will give it time to contract slightly away from the sides of the pan.

5. Then slide it out, on its side, onto a wooden board. Pick it up and stand it upright on a cooling rack. Eat it while it's very fresh.

If the flour to liquid ratio doesn't seem quite right for your machine, in that the amount of liquid seems too great, try increasing the flour measurement to 500g and decrease the water to 260ml. Check with your machine's instruction booklet recipes to see the typical flour to liquid ratio for your machine.

2
Dough Recipes

Whilst it's wonderful to have your bread machine bake the whole loaf for you from beginning to end and produce a finished loaf – particularly during a busy working week – it's also extremely rewarding (and much more fun) to explore all the options and opportunities the **Dough** programmes can offer you. When you are not quite so rushed, perhaps over the weekend, you can take the time to create your own oven-baked loaves, rolls, buns and pizzas. Perhaps more unexpectedly, you can also use your bread machine to make tortillas, pancakes, pasta and even marzipan (see the Cake section).

PROGRAMMES

Your machine will have a selection of different programmes, usually including:

- ◆ a **Basic Dough** programme which is useful for the majority of doughs you will make;

- ◆ a **Raisin Dough** option which is useful for when you are adding dried fruit and so on where the pieces are to remain whole rather than broken up and incorporated into the mixture;

- a **French Dough** programme, which is longer and allows doughs extra time to develop, giving a more open texture and yeasty flavour;
- a **Whole wheat Dough** programme that is also longer and allows the gluten more time to develop. It may also spend time at the beginning of the cycle gently warming the ingredients to help with gluten development;
- a **Pizza Dough** programme, which is a short dough cycle that's perfect for pizza bases. You can also use this one for pasta, tortilla and pancake recipes.

ORDER OF INGREDIENTS

When adding the ingredients to the bread pan, the most important aspect to bear in mind is to keep the yeast dry and away from the salt and sugar in the very first stages.

The preferred method for adding ingredients is usually to put the liquid in first, the salt and the sugar spaced apart, then the flour and the yeast on top last of all. This works well with most machines and is particularly helpful with the occasional machine that struggles slightly to gather up all the flour into the dough ball during the initial mixing.

If in doubt, add the ingredients in the order specified by your instruction book.

KNEADING AND PROVING OR RISING

Assuming you have all the correct ingredients in the correct proportions and your oven is working properly, the two main reasons for home-made bread not succeeding are not enough kneading and not enough rising time. This isn't a worry with loaves baked entirely in the bread machine – the machine will take care of everything – but if you are making bread by hand, or even making bread using dough made in the machine, then it's important to bear these things in mind.

With regard to dough made in the bread machine, it will already have been kneaded and the gluten encouraged to develop, but another kneading from you, once the dough is out of the machine and before it is shaped, will improve the texture still further as the kneading action encourages further gluten development and also knocks out any large air bubbles that may have formed – these air bubbles aren't a huge problem but can lead to a few large 'holes' in the finished bread that you might prefer to be without.

KNEADING TECHNIQUES

As mentioned, with dough that's already kneaded in the bread machine you don't actually have to be too vigorous with your own kneading. However, another important aspect of kneading is that it is actually extremely enjoyable and fun to do. If you can remember happy hours as a child spent modelling with Plasticine and Play-Doh, then you'll be glad to know you can have many more now you are all grown up, playing with bread dough – *and* it is cleaner and smells much better!

You will develop your own kneading technique as you go along but start off with a basic pushing, rolling and folding action. Roll the dough into a ball and then attempt to flatten it while pushing it away from you. Fold it over and fold it over again. Repeat this several times then roll it into a ball and start again. You can also roll it into a long sausage and fold it back on itself. You might like to use the heels of your hands and even your lower forearms as you knead. Clench both fists and roll and push the dough.

Kneading is the action of stretching the gluten strands, so incorporate plenty of pulling and stretching into your technique. Imagine the gluten strands as pieces of elastic that grow stronger each time they are pulled taut and then released. Once the dough starts to feel smooth and silky, with quite a bit of bounce and give, you are there.

While kneading and moulding you will need a small amount of flour on your work surface, and probably on your hands if the dough is a little sticky, but try to keep it to a minimum.

PROVING OR RISING

Although with bread machine dough you don't have to be too vigorous with kneading, *it is absolutely essential that you allow your bread to prove or rise* (they mean the same thing in this context) *once it has been moulded and positioned in the tin or on the baking tray.* It's difficult to say how long this should be for –

perhaps an hour or two – as it depends entirely on the ambient temperature; dough will rise more slowly if the room is cold, more quickly if it is hot. Having said that, bread that has risen *too* quickly isn't generally as good as that which has taken more time: you need to find a balance.

Generally speaking, ready-for-the-oven dough should have almost doubled in size but still look fairly sleek and firm – if it starts to look a little too light and stretched, and seem on the point of collapse, it has proved for too long.

RISING OUT OF THE OVEN AND RISING IN THE OVEN

It's worth remembering that while cakes do all their rising in the oven, bread does the majority of its rising before it gets into the oven. When bread first gets into the oven it then has a final spurt of rising, known as 'oven spring'.

FLOUR TO LIQUID RATIOS

An alternative amount of flour and liquid is suggested for some recipes. The second amount may be better suited to the more competitively priced makes of bread machine, which tend to use a greater proportion of flour to liquid.

Mixtures containing significant quantities of moist fruit or vegetable such as apple, banana and so on, tend to perform successfully in most types of machine without altering the original amounts of flour and liquid in the mixture. The final amount of dough may be slightly smaller in volume when made in the more competitively priced machines.

Richer, brioche-type mixtures containing generous quantities of butter and egg also tend to perform successfully in most types of machine without altering the original amounts of flour and liquid in the mixture. Again, the final amount of dough may be slightly smaller in volume when made in the more competitively priced machines.

Always use the measuring spoon that comes with your bread machine for both dry and liquid ingredients; and always fill the spoons to the top and level off dry ingredients.

Bread Rolls

Main recipe

One of the best things about the dough programmes is being able to make your own bread rolls. Here is the basic recipe which you can adapt in a variety of ways.

Makes 12

330ml water	1 tablespoon sugar
2 tablespoons mild oil	500g strong white bread flour
1 teaspoon salt	1½ teaspoons quick yeast

You will need a large greased baking tray

1. Pour the water and oil into the bread pan of your machine and add the salt and sugar, placing them at different ends of the pan.

2. Put the flour on top and finally the yeast. Select the **Basic Dough** programme.

3. Once the dough is ready, turn it out onto a floured board, knead it briefly and cut the dough into 12 equal pieces.

4. Mould the pieces into rounds: roll each one between your cupped hands until you have a smooth ball. When you first mould each piece you may hear a faint tell-tale squeak as air escapes.

5. Space them out evenly on the baking tray and leave to prove until almost doubled in size.

6. Bake in a preheated oven at 180–220°C (fan oven) or equivalent, for 9–10 minutes or until golden brown.

7. Remove and cool on a wire rack. A clean tea towel over the top will keep the rolls fresh and moist as they cool.

If the flour to liquid ratio doesn't seem quite right for your machine, in that the amount of liquid seems too great, try increasing the flour measurement to 550g and decreasing the water to 290ml. Check with your machine's instruction booklet recipes to see the typical flour to liquid ratio for your machine.

Dividing dough into 12 equal pieces

As a rough guide, form your dough into a ball and flatten the top until you have more of a cake shape. Cut the dough into quarters with a sharp knife.

Take each quarter and cut it into three equal wedges, as if you were slicing a cake into three equal pieces. Mould each piece into a ball.

Freezing rolls

It's handy to have a couple of bags of home-baked rolls in the freezer for contingencies. Make sure the rolls are completely cold and seal them inside a freezer-grade bag, taking care to exclude all the air.

To defrost

Remove the rolls from the freezer bag and defrost them on a plate, covered by a clean tea towel, at room temperature. You can defrost these in the microwave but it's terribly easy to overdo it and if you are not careful they can end up starting to cook and harden.

Most freezer manufacturers suggest freezing bread for up to three months but check with your own freezer manufacturer's recommendations.

Adding other flours to the main recipe

Once you have got the hang of the basic roll recipe you might like to try experimenting with adding other types of flour. You could replace half of the white flour with wholemeal. Alternatively, you could replace 75–100g of white flour with spelt flour or buckwheat or rye. Malted grain and barleycorn mixes are also good. Alternatively, try kamut flour. Like spelt flour, this is another ancient wheat-type grain: it is particularly high in selenium, which many modern diets can lack, and has a lovely sweet taste.

Baps

using main recipe

To make baps, prepare the dough as for the main recipe but mould into flatter rounds. As the finishing touch, dust the baked baps with a little flour stirred through a tea-strainer with a teaspoon for an even distribution.

Sesame Seed Buns

using main recipe

You can make classic burger buns by making bap shapes and brushing the risen baps with water and sprinkling with sesame seeds just before they go into the oven.

Round of Rolls

using main recipe

You can make a most attractive and professional-looking round loaf that looks as though it would be at home in a high-class baker's window – or prominently displayed at the Harvest Festival – by shaping the dough into 12 rounds and arranging them in a greased 23cm round loose-bottomed cake tin.

1. Once the dough is ready, turn it out onto a floured board, knead it briefly and cut the dough into 12 equal pieces.

2. Mould the dough into 12 balls and arrange nine round the outside in a ring and three in the middle. Leave to prove until almost doubled in size and joined together.

3. If you are feeling fancy, once they have risen and just before you put them in the oven, you could brush them lightly with water and top some with poppy seeds, some with sesame seeds and some with porridge oats for a professional-looking finishing touch.

4. Bake in a preheated oven at 180–220°C (fan oven) or equivalent for around 30 minutes or until golden brown.

5. Leave to settle for a while and then remove in one piece and cool on a wire rack. A clean tea towel placed over the top will keep the round fresh and moist as it cools.

6. Alternatively, if your rolls are made with white flour, you could dust them with a little flour once they come out of the oven: stir the flour through a tea strainer with a teaspoon for an even distribution.

'Rise to Fit' Rolls in a Bun Tin

using main recipe

These rolls have a really appealing shape, very like little 'flowerpot' loaves, and are very easy to make.

You will need a greased 12-cup muffin tin

1. Once the dough is ready, turn it out onto a floured board, knead it briefly and cut the dough into 12 equal pieces.

2. Roll each piece lightly in the flour on the board and mould the dough into rounds: roll each piece between your cupped hands until you have a smooth ball and arrange in the prepared muffin tin. Leave to prove until almost doubled in size.

3. Preheat the oven to 180–220°C (fan oven) or equivalent and bake the rolls for 8–10 minutes until golden.

Baby Rolls in a Bun Tin

using main recipe

Try dividing the dough into 24 and baking the rolls in two mini-muffin tins. Baking time is about the same as for the larger ones but keep an eye on them: they may need to come out of the oven a fraction earlier. These are great for children although the downside is – they disappear virtually as soon as they come out of the oven.

Rolls in Frills

using main recipe

These are appealing to look at and a little bit different. The paper cases make the rolls look very cute but they also have a practical purpose in that they act as a kind of corset to make the dough rise in a more uniform domed shape. Don't forget to dip the pieces of dough in oil as directed or you'll find it tricky peeling the paper cases off the finished rolls.

You will need a 12-cup muffin tin lined with muffin-size paper cases and a small saucer of mild oil

1. Prepare the rolls as for the main recipe.

2. Dip each ball of dough to about halfway up in the oil, shake off any excess and put into the paper cases in the muffin tin. This will prevent the rolls sticking to the paper cases once baked. Leave to prove until almost doubled in size.

3. Preheat the oven to 180–220°C (fan oven) or equivalent and bake the rolls for 8–10 minutes until golden.

4. Dust the rolls with a little flour once they come out of the oven: stir the flour through a tea strainer with a teaspoon for an even distribution.

Mini-loaf Rolls

using main recipe

Mini-loaf tins, the kind you can buy in packs of four, usually with a non-stick finish, are brilliant for making appealing bread rolls that look like little mini loaves. If you are entertaining, and have the time, you could make a batch of **Rolls in a Bun Tin** and a batch of **Mini-loaf Rolls**, using white dough for one kind and wholemeal dough or mixed grain for the other.

You will need 12 greased mini-loaf tins and a baking tray

1. Make the dough as for the main recipe. If you wish, replace 75–100g of white flour with malted grain, barleycorn, spelt flour, buckwheat, rye or kamut flour.

2. Once the dough is ready, take it out of the machine. Put the dough onto a floured surface, knead it briefly and cut into 12 equal pieces.

3. Put a piece into each prepared mini-loaf tin, turning each piece to reveal a smooth top. Place the tins on a baking tray; this will make it easier to lift them in and out of the oven. Leave to prove until almost doubled in size.

4. Bake in a preheated oven at your usual bread temperature of 180–220°C (fan oven) or equivalent for approximately 8–10 minutes.

5. Once baked, leave in the tin to cool and contract for a few minutes. You should then be able to just lift them out of the tins. Cool on a wire rack.

PROPER CARE AND PROLONGING THE LIFE OF YOUR MINI-LOAF TINS

It's not cheap to build up a stock of 12 mini-loaf tins so be sure to look after them carefully to keep them in good condition. Instead of scrubbing them in hot soapy water or throwing them into the dishwasher, it's usually possible to clean them perfectly well by wiping with kitchen paper.

Don't poke about with a metal knife when trying to remove bread and cakes. Allow items to cool for a few moments and contract away from the sides of the tin and they should then lift out easily. If something does get stuck, use a sturdy plastic picnic knife to ease it out.

Barm Cakes

True barm cakes from the north of England have a strong yeasty flavour and were originally made with beer barm: a natural leaven and by-product from the beer industry. This version of barm cakes is similar to a bap, but with a 'yeastier' and more flavoursome dough. This is achieved, in this case, not by using beer barm but by using a longer dough programme to allow the yeasty flavour to develop. In times gone by, people would go to the local brewery for a jug of brewer's yeast. These days, yeast is made on a large scale in dedicated factories. Lightly dust the baked barms with flour for a traditional finish. These are a great all-round roll for any time of day and they are especially good split, lightly buttered and filled with freshly cooked chips for the perfect chip buttie.

Makes 8

300ml water	10g lard or block vegetable shortening
400g strong white bread flour	1 teaspoon quick yeast
1 teaspoon salt	1 tablespoon sugar

1. Put the water and lard or vegetable shortening into the bread pan of your machine and add the salt and sugar, placing them at different ends of the pan. Put the flour on top and finally the yeast. Select the **French Dough** programme (or your longest dough programme).

2. Once the dough is ready, put it onto a floured board, knead it briefly and divide into eight equal pieces. Roll each piece into a ball between your cupped hands and flatten slightly into a disc shape. Transfer to the prepared baking tray until almost doubled in size.

3. Bake in a preheated oven at 180–220°C (fan oven) or equivalent for approximately 20 minutes.

4. Cool on a wire rack. A clean tea towel placed over the top will keep the barm cakes fresh and moist inside as they cool. You may like to dust them lightly with flour before serving.

If the flour to liquid ratio doesn't seem quite right for your machine, in that the amount of liquid seems too great, try increasing the total flour measurement to 500g land decrease the water to 260ml. Check with your machine's instruction booklet recipes to see the typical flour to liquid ratio for your machine.

Egg and Chip Barm

Try filling a lightly buttered barm with chips and sitting a fried egg on top. Put the lid on and squash down slightly for a satisfying cross between a chip buttie and a fried egg sandwich.

Large Baguettes

These baguettes have a softer crumb than an authentic French baguette but they have a lovely crisp and chewy crust. Bake them early for a Continental breakfast to have with coffee, unsalted butter and some decent jam, or serve with a selection of cheeses or sausages and mustard for a convivial lunch.

Makes 2

300ml water	400g strong white bread flour
1 teaspoon salt	1 teaspoon quick yeast
1 tablespoon sugar	

1. Pour the water into the bread pan of your machine and add the salt and sugar, placing them at different ends of the pan. Put the flour on top and finally the yeast.

2. Select the **French Dough** programme (or your longest dough programme).

3. Once the dough is ready, put it on to a floured board, knead it briefly and divide into two.

4. Roll each piece into a cylinder and leave on the prepared baking tray until almost doubled in size.

5. Slash the top of the baguettes – you can make several diagonal slashes or one long one down the centre – with a sharp knife. This releases any air trapped in the bread so the baguette doesn't balloon out of shape.

6. Since many of us are unlikely to have the benefit of a commercial steam-injected oven, put a wide ovenproof dish of water on the bottom oven shelf before you preheat the oven – the steam will set the outside of the bread so that it bakes hard and produces a crispy crust.

7. Alternatively, for nicely puffed up baguettes with a softer crumb and a chewy rather than a crisp crust, bake them without the steam and don't slash the tops.

8. Bake on a greased baking tray in a preheated oven at 180-220°C (fan oven) or equivalent for approximately 20-25 minutes.

9. Cool on a wire rack.

10. If you prefer, mould the dough into one large baguette and bake in the same way for approximately 25 minutes.

If the flour to liquid ratio doesn't seem quite right for your machine, in that the amount of liquid seems too great, try increasing the total flour measurement to 500g and decrease the water to 260ml. Check with your machine's instruction booklet recipes to see the typical flour to liquid ratio for your machine.

Small Baguettes

Alternatively, you can buy special grooved and perforated trays to bake small baguettes on. They usually hold three baguettes at a time and although probably never used by a genuine French baker, are very helpful for making authentic-looking baguettes at home.

Makes 3 or 6

You will need a greased baking tray or a perforated baguette tray (there should be no need to grease this)

1. Prepare the dough as for the previous recipe.

2. Once the dough is ready, put it onto a floured board, knead it briefly and divide into three.

3. You can make three smallish baguettes or divide each piece further into two to make six even smaller ones.

4. Roll each piece into a cylinder and arrange on the baking or baguette tray. Leave to prove until almost doubled in size – if using a perforated tray, the baguettes should be perfectly happy to prove on this.

5. See the previous recipe for instructions on introducing steam and slashing the tops.

6. Bake in a preheated oven at 180-220°C (fan oven) or equivalent for approximately 10 minutes until golden brown.

7. Cool on a wire rack. A clean tea towel placed over the top will keep the baguettes fresh and moist as they cool.

Garlic Bread and Garlic Toast

Garlic Bread

Baguettes make excellent garlic bread. Slice into generous chunks and spread each chunk on both sides with **garlic butter**. Piece the baguette back together and wrap in foil. Bake at 180–220°C (fan oven) or equivalent for about 20 minutes and then open the foil, separate the slices slightly, and return to the oven for a further 5 minutes or so.

Very Quick Garlic Toast

This is very quick and easy. Use any bread you have to hand, although white is more traditional for garlic bread, and slice fairly thickly.

Mix some **softened butter** with some **finely sliced garlic clove** or a little **minced garlic from a jar**. Lightly toast the bread. Allow the toast to cool slightly and spread with the garlic butter. Cut each slice into two diagonally and serve immediately.

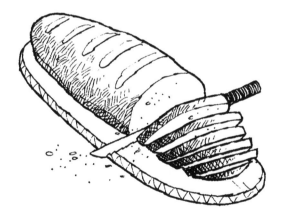

Wholemeal Loaf

This has a beautifully sweet, nutty taste and is nourishing and extremely satisfying – which is after all the whole point of bread. There is a little extra water in this recipe as wholemeal flour tends to absorb more liquid than white.

320ml warm water

2 tablespoons mild oil

1 teaspoon salt

1 tablespoon sugar

400g strong wholemeal bread flour

1 teaspoon quick yeast

You will need a greased 450g loaf tin

1. Pour the water and oil into the bread pan of your machine and add the salt and sugar, placing them at different ends of the pan. Put the flour on top and finally the yeast. Select the **Whole wheat Dough** programme.

2. Once the dough is ready, remove it from the machine with lightly floured hands and knead it briefly on a lightly floured work surface.

3. Mould it into an approximate oval shape and put it into the prepared loaf tin. Leave to prove until it has almost doubled in size.

4. Bake in a preheated oven at your usual bread temperature of 180–220°C (fan oven) or equivalent for approximately 20–25 minutes or until light brown all over.

If the flour to liquid ratio doesn't seem quite right for your machine, in that the amount of liquid seems too great, try increasing the total flour measurement to 500g and decrease the water to 280ml. Check with your machine's instruction booklet recipes to see the typical flour to liquid ratio for your machine.

Wholemeal Bread Bun

Although made with a cultivated modern strain of flour that has been finely milled, this loaf is approaching the style of most people's daily bread centuries ago. It's a simple hand-formed wheat cake that could have been baked on the hearth. The sugar and oil are modern additions.

320ml warm water	1 tablespoon sugar
2 tablespoons mild oil	400g strong wholemeal bread flour
1 teaspoon salt	1 teaspoon quick yeast

You will need a large greased baking tray

1. Pour the water and oil into the bread pan of your machine and add the salt and sugar, placing them at different ends of the pan. Put the flour on top and finally the yeast. Select the **Whole wheat Dough** programme.

2. Once the dough is ready, remove it from the machine with lightly floured hands and knead it briefly on a lightly floured work surface.

3. Mould it into a round. Use one hand and roll it round your work surface until you get the right flattish bun shape.

4. Place on the prepared baking tray and leave to prove until it has almost doubled in size.

5. Bake in a preheated oven at your usual bread temperature of 180–220°C (fan oven) or equivalent for approximately 25 minutes or until light brown all over.

If the flour to liquid ratio doesn't seem quite right for your machine, in that the amount of liquid seems too great, try increasing the total flour measurement to 500g and decrease the water to 280ml. Check with your machine's instruction booklet recipes to see the typical flour to liquid ratio for your machine.

Half and Half Hovis Loaf

Main recipe

This is very like the 'small brown loaf' you might have popped out to the baker's shop to buy years ago.

320ml warm water	200g strong white bread flour
2 tablespoons mild oil	200g Hovis bread flour
1 teaspoon salt	1 teaspoon quick yeast
1 tablespoon sugar	

You will need a greased 450g loaf tin

1. Pour the water and oil into the bread pan of your machine and add the salt and sugar, placing them at different ends of the pan. Put the flours on top and finally the yeast. Select the **Basic Dough** programme.

2. Once the dough is ready, remove it from the machine with lightly floured hands and knead it briefly on a lightly floured work surface.

3. Mould it into an approximate oval shape and put it into the prepared tin. Leave to prove until almost doubled in size.

4. Preheat your oven to your usual bread-baking temperature of 180–220°C (fan oven) or equivalent and bake for around 25–30 minutes until golden brown.

5. Leave to settle and contract away from the sides of the tin for a few minutes and then transfer to a wire rack to cool.

If the flour to liquid ratio doesn't seem quite right for your machine, in that the amount of liquid seems too great, try increasing the total flour measurement to 500g and decrease the water to 270ml. Check with your machine's instruction booklet recipes to see the typical flour to liquid ratio for your machine.

Half and Half Hovis Mini Loaves

Makes 12 mini loaves

You will need 12 greased mini-loaf tins (the kind you can buy in packs of four)

1. Make the dough as for the previous recipe. Select the **Dough** setting.

2. Once the dough is ready, take it out of the machine, put it onto a floured surface and knead it briefly.

3. Cut into 12 equal pieces and put a piece into each prepared mini-loaf tin, turning each to reveal a smooth top. Place the tins on a baking tray to make it easier to lift them in and out of the oven. Leave to prove until almost doubled in size.

4. Bake in a preheated oven at your usual bread temperature of 180–220°C (fan oven) or equivalent for approximately 8–10 minutes.

5. Once baked, leave in the tin to cool and contract for a few minutes. You should then be able to just lift them out of the tins.

Crusty Farmhouse Loaf

This is a delicious loaf with an old-fashioned look about it.

300ml warm water	1 tablespoon sugar
2 tablespoons mild oil	400g strong white bread flour
1 teaspoon salt	1 teaspoon quick yeast

You will need a greased 450g loaf tin

1. Pour the water and oil into the bread pan of your machine and add the salt and sugar, placing them at different ends of the pan. Put the flour on top and finally the yeast. Select the **Basic Dough** programme.

2. Once the dough is ready, remove it from the machine with lightly floured hands and knead it briefly on a lightly floured work surface.

3. Mould it into an approximate oval shape and put it into the prepared tin. Leave it to prove until it has almost doubled in size.

4. Once it has risen sufficiently, dust the top with a little flour stirred through a tea strainer and, using your sharpest non-serrated knife, make a deep cut lengthwise across the top.

5. Turn the oven on to its highest temperature and leave the loaf until the oven has come to temperature.

6. Put the loaf in the oven and, as soon as you have shut the door, turn the oven down to the temperature you would normally use to bake bread, 180–220°C or equivalent. Bake for approximately 30 minutes until browned and ready.

7. Remove from the oven and leave for a few minutes for the loaf to cool and contract slightly before you turn it out. Cool on a wire rack.

If the flour to liquid ratio doesn't seem quite right for your machine, in that the amount of liquid seems too great, try increasing the total flour measurement to 500g and decrease the water to 260ml. Check with your machine's instruction booklet recipes to see the typical flour to liquid ratio for your machine.

Large Flat Bread Bun

This is exactly the same dough as the **Crusty Farmhouse Loaf** above but is baked as a flat round on a baking tray and comes out with a much softer and more delicate crust. It is so simple to make and easy to slice. If you make bread regularly, this might be the one you'll make again and again.

300ml warm water	1 tablespoon sugar
2 tablespoons mild oil	400g strong white bread flour
1 teaspoon salt	1 teaspoon quick yeast

You will need a large greased baking tray

1. Pour the water and oil into the bread pan of your machine and add the salt and sugar, placing them at different ends of the pan. Put the flour on top and finally the yeast. Select the **Basic Dough** programme.

2. Once the dough is ready, remove it from the machine with lightly floured hands and knead it briefly on a lightly floured work surface.

3. Mould it into a round. Use one hand and roll it round your work surface until you get the right flattish bun shape. Ease it onto the prepared baking tray and leave to prove until it has almost doubled in size.

4. Bake in a preheated oven at your usual bread temperature of 180–220°C (fan oven) or equivalent for approximately 20–25 minutes or until light brown all over.

5. Leave on the tray for a few moments and transfer to a wire rack to cool. A clean tea towel over the top will keep the bun moist as it cools.

6. You may like to dust the bun very lightly with flour (stir a little through a tea strainer with a teaspoon) before you serve it.

If the flour to liquid ratio doesn't seem quite right for your machine, in that the amount of liquid seems too great, try increasing the total flour measurement to 500g and decrease the water to 260ml. Check with your machine's instruction booklet recipes to see the typical flour to liquid ratio for your machine.

Plain White Loaf

Here is a perfectly plain and simple, no-nonsense loaf. It contains just the four basic bread ingredients of flour and water, yeast and salt. It has a beautiful flavour and a slightly rougher texture than bread containing fat or oil. It also makes very good toast. You may find it doesn't keep quite as well as a loaf that contains oil.

300ml warm water   400g strong white bread flour
1 teaspoon salt   1 teaspoon quick yeast

You will need a greased 450g loaf tin

1. Pour the water into the bread pan of your machine and add the salt. Put the flour on top and finally the yeast. Select the **Basic Dough** programme.

2. Once the dough is ready, remove it from the machine with lightly floured hands and knead it briefly on a lightly floured work surface.

3. Mould it into an approximate oval shape and put it into the prepared loaf tin. Leave to prove until it has almost doubled in size.

4. Bake in a preheated oven at your usual bread temperature of 180-220°C (fan oven) or equivalent for approximately 20–25 minutes or until light brown all over.

If the flour to liquid ratio doesn't seem quite right for your machine, in that the amount of liquid seems too great, try increasing the total flour measurement to 500g and decrease the water to 260ml. Check with your machine's instruction booklet recipes to see the typical flour to liquid ratio for your machine.

Plain and Simple Large Flat White Bread Bun

Here is a perfectly plain and simple, round bread bun. This is the simplest and most traditional type of loaf. It contains just the four basic bread ingredients of flour and water, yeast and salt and needs no tin, just a baking tray. Generations ago, it could have been baked on the hearthstone, although not from such pure, white, modern flour.

300ml warm water	400g strong white bread flour
1 teaspoon salt	1 teaspoon quick yeast

You will need a large greased baking tray

1. Pour the water into the bread pan of your machine and add the salt. Put the flour on top and finally the yeast. Select the **Basic Dough** programme.

2. Once the dough is ready, remove it from the machine with lightly floured hands and knead it briefly on a lightly floured work surface.

3. Mould it into a round. Use one hand and roll it round your work surface until you get the right flattish bun shape.

4. Ease it onto the prepared baking tray and leave to prove until it has almost doubled in size.

5. Bake in a preheated oven at your usual bread temperature of 180–220°C (fan oven) or equivalent for approximately 20–25 minutes or until light brown all over.

If the flour to liquid ratio doesn't seem quite right for your machine, in that the amount of liquid seems too great, try increasing the total flour measurement to 500g and decrease the water to 260ml. Check with your machine's instruction booklet recipes to see the typical flour to liquid ratio for your machine.

Cottage Loaf

This old-fashioned-looking classic crusty loaf is the kind that often appears on the table in children's storybooks for a 'slap-up' farmhouse tea.

275ml lukewarm water or milk	1 tablespoon sugar
3 tablespoons mild oil	500g strong white bread flour
1 teaspoon salt	1 teaspoons quick yeast

You will need a large greased baking tray

1. Pour the water and oil into the bread pan of your machine and add the salt and sugar, placing them at different ends of the pan. Put the flour on top and finally the yeast, positioning it on top. Select the **Basic Dough** programme.

2. Once the dough is ready, remove it from the machine with lightly floured hands and knead it briefly on a lightly floured work surface.

3. Divide the dough into two pieces: one piece should be about two thirds of the mixture or a fraction more and the other about one third or a fraction less.

4. Roll the larger piece into a ball and put it towards one end of your prepared tray, but allowing it sufficient room all round to rise. Roll the smaller piece into a ball and place it on the tray as far away from the other piece as you can – again, while still leaving enough space all the way round for it to rise. If they won't both fit on the baking tray you will need to use a second tray for this stage, although this second tray doesn't need to be an ovenproof baking tray. Leave the dough in a warm place to prove until it has almost doubled in size.

5. When the dough has risen, manoeuvre the smaller piece on top of the larger one; make sure it is positioned nicely in the middle. (Incidentally, if you assemble the loaf *before* it has risen, you won't have the two clear parts to the loaf – it will all merge into one big amorphous mass.)

6. Grease the handle of a wooden spoon and plunge the greased handle through the centre of the ball on top of the loaf right through until it

touches the baking tray. Ease it out again gently. This will leave you with a nice little dimple on top and anchor the 'topknot' securely onto the loaf.

7. Alternatively, you can use your finger or, for a flatter loaf that looks more 'of a piece', you can use the thumb and forefinger of both hands at the same time. With your thumbs in the centre and your fingers positioned on either side of the loaf, work round, making quite a large hole.

8. Leave the loaf to rise a little longer while you preheat your oven to its highest temperature.

9. When the oven has come to temperature, put in your loaf, turn the oven down to 180-220°C and bake for 30 minutes or so until golden brown.

10. Cool on a wire rack: a clean tea towel over the top will keep it moist as it cools.

If the flour to liquid ratio doesn't seem quite right for your machine, in that the amount of liquid seems too great, try decreasing the water to 260ml. This will result in a slightly smaller loaf. Check with your machine's instruction booklet recipes to see the typical flour to liquid ratio for your machine.

Novelty Duck Rolls

You can make these for a children's tea party; they are really cute and look like little bath ducks. The duck part is really simple to put together: if you aren't normally very artistic you will stun yourself with your sudden expertise!

Makes 12 rolls

Dough as for **Cottage Loaf**   1 or 2 carrots, peeled
24 currants

You will need a large greased baking tray

1. Make the dough as above. Flour your hands and transfer the dough to a lightly floured board. Knead briefly and divide the dough into two pieces: one piece should be about two thirds of the mixture or a fraction more and the other about one third or a fraction less.

2. Divide the larger piece into 12 equal pieces and mould gently into flattish rounds – as if you were making small baps – and space them out in their final positions on the prepared baking tray.

3. Divide the smaller piece into 12 and mould into round balls between your cupped hands.

   Space them out well onto a second well-greased tray – you will need enough room between them when they are fully risen to manoeuvre them off the tray with a palette knife.

4. Leave them all in a warm place for 40 minutes or so until they have risen and virtually doubled in size. If you can cover both sets of dough with an upturned bowl or something similar, it will stop them drying out.

5. Position the round balls on top of the flatter rolls. Put them in the middle; they will drift of their own accord while baking to more of a 'head' position. Leave them to rise a little longer while you preheat your oven to 180–220°C (fan ovens) or equivalent.

6. When the oven has come to temperature, put the rolls in and bake for 8 minutes or so until golden. Leave on the tray for a few moments before

transferring to a wire rack to cool. A clean tea towel placed over the top will keep them moist as they cool.

7. Once they are cool, make tiny slits either side of each 'head' for eyes and wedge the currants into position. Make a longer slit where each beak will be and cut beak shapes from the peeled carrot. Wedge into position.

Don't be surprised if some of your more sensitive guests haven't quite got the heart to eat the duck rolls!

Milk Loaf

A milk loaf isn't massively different from a regular white loaf but it does have a lovely extra soft and fine texture. Use skimmed milk for a slightly softer, finer texture. Milk loaves keep well but they are at their softest and most delicious when fresh.

300ml warm skimmed milk	1 tablespoon sugar
2 tablespoons mild oil	400g strong white bread flour
1 teaspoon salt	1 teaspoon quick yeast

You will need a greased 450g loaf tin

1. Pour the skimmed milk and oil into the bread pan of your machine and add the salt and sugar, placing them at different ends of the pan. Put the flour on top and finally the yeast. Select the **Basic Dough** programme.

2. Once the dough is ready, remove it from the machine with lightly floured hands and knead it briefly on a lightly floured work surface.

3. Mould it into an oval shape and put it into the prepared tin. Leave to prove until it has almost doubled in size.

4. Bake in a preheated oven at your usual bread temperature of 180-220°C (fan oven) or equivalent for approximately 20-25 minutes or until light brown all over.

If the flour to liquid ratio doesn't seem quite right for your machine, in that the amount of liquid seems too great, try increasing the total flour measurement to 500g and decrease the milk to 260ml. Check with your machine's instruction booklet recipes to see the typical flour to liquid ratio for your machine.

Mini Milk Loaves

Milk loaf dough makes lovely little mini loaves baked in mini-loaf tins. These are really popular with small children, both to eat at mealtimes or to cut into dinky little slices for dolls' and teddy bears' tea parties.

Makes 12 mini loaves

300ml warm skimmed milk	1 tablespoon sugar
2 tablespoons mild oil	400g strong white bread flour
1 teaspoon salt	1 teaspoon quick yeast

You will need 12 greased mini-loaf tins

1. Pour the skimmed milk and oil into the bread pan of your machine and add the salt and sugar, placing them at different ends of the pan. Put the flour on top and finally the yeast, positioning it on top. Select the **Basic Dough** programme.

2. Once the dough is ready, take it out of the machine, put it onto a floured surface and knead it briefly.

3. Cut into 12 equal pieces and put a piece into each prepared mini-loaf tin, turning each to reveal a smooth top. Place the tins on a baking tray to make it easier to lift them in and out of the oven. Leave to prove until almost doubled in size.

4. Bake in a preheated oven at your usual bread temperature of 180–220°C (fan oven) or equivalent for approximately 8–10 minutes.

5. Once baked, leave in the tin to cool and contract for a few minutes. You should then be able to just lift them out of the tins.

If the flour to liquid ratio doesn't seem quite right for your machine, in that the amount of liquid seems too great, try increasing the total flour measurement to 500g and decrease the milk to 260ml. Check with your machine's instruction booklet recipes to see the typical flour to liquid ratio for your machine.

Milk Splits

This is the same dough as for the **Milk Loaf** and **Mini Milk Loaves,** above, but baked like this they are very like Devonshire or Cornish Splits: soft white rolls split and eaten with clotted cream and jam. They make a lovely alternative to scones.

If you are going to eat them like this, sieve a little white flour (or icing sugar if you prefer) over the top of each one using a teaspoon and a small sieve or tea strainer. Eat them while they are very fresh.

Makes 12 rolls

300ml warm skimmed milk	1 tablespoon sugar
2 tablespoons mild oil	400g strong white bread flour
1 teaspoon salt	1 teaspoon quick yeast

You will need a greased 12-cup muffin tin

1. Pour the milk and oil into the bread pan of your machine and add the salt and sugar, placing them at different ends of the pan. Put the flour on top and finally the yeast, positioning it on top. Select the **Basic Dough** programme.

2. Once the dough is ready, turn it out onto a floured board and cut the dough into 12 equal pieces. There is no need to knock it back or knead it further.

3. Roll each piece lightly in the flour on the board and mould the dough into rounds: roll each piece between your cupped hands until you have a smooth ball and arrange in the prepared muffin tin. Leave them in a warm place for an hour or so until doubled in size.

4. Bake in a preheated oven at 180-220°C (fan oven) or equivalent, for 8-10 minutes until golden brown. Leave on the baking tray for a few moments to cool and contract and then remove and finish cooling on a wire rack. A clean tea towel placed over the top will keep the rolls fresh and moist as they cool.

5. Dust each roll with a little flour (or icing sugar); stir it through a tea strainer for a light, even distribution

If the flour to liquid ratio doesn't seem quite right for your machine, in that the amount of liquid seems too great, try increasing the total flour measurement to 500g and decrease the milk to 260ml. Check with your machine's instruction booklet recipes to see the typical flour to liquid ratio for your machine.

Bridge Rolls

Who knows why bridge rolls are called *bridge* rolls? Is it because they are shaped like a bridge, or maybe because they are sometimes served at card parties? Whatever the origin of the name, they are a really useful-shaped roll to be able to make. You can serve them at teatime filled with cheese, ham, egg, potted meats or fish pastes and so on, and they are also perfect for accommodating a sausage. A hot sausage in a bridge roll is great for children's parties, or take them filled with a cold sausage to picnics.

Makes 12 rolls

300ml warm water	1 tablespoon sugar
2 tablespoons mild oil	400g strong white bread flour
1 teaspoon salt	1 teaspoon quick yeast

You will need a large greased baking tray

1. Pour the water and oil into the bread pan of your machine and add the salt and sugar, placing them at different ends of the pan. Put the flour on top and finally the yeast, positioning it on top. Select the **Basic Dough** programme.

2. Once the dough is ready, turn it out onto a lightly floured board and cut the dough into four equal pieces. You may need to add a little more flour as you go along, but try to keep it to a minimum.

3. Working with one piece on the board at a time, to give yourself elbow room, roll a piece into a long cylinder shape. Cut the cylinder into three equal pieces.

4. Take one of the pieces and roll it on the board with the flat of your hand. Try to roll with your three middle fingers, lightly backwards and forwards, and then gently tuck in the ends of the roll with your thumb and little finger as you do so. Repeat with each piece until you have 12 rolls.

5. Lay the rolls on the prepared baking tray in two rows of six, fairly close together, so that they will touch each other as they spread out and you'll have two joined rows of six rolls each. Leave them in a warm place for an hour or so until doubled in size.

6. Bake in a preheated oven at 180–220°C (fan oven) or equivalent, for 8–10 minutes or until golden brown.

7. Leave on the baking tray for a few moments to cool slightly and then remove and finish cooling on a wire rack. A clean tea towel placed over the top will keep the rolls fresh and moist as they cool.

8. Eat these very fresh to enjoy them at their best.

See also **Iced Buns** in Chapter 3, 'Sweet Loaves, Buns and Tea Breads'.

If the flour to liquid ratio doesn't seem quite right for your machine, in that the amount of liquid seems too great, try increasing the total flour measurement to 500g and decrease the water to 260ml. Check with your machine's instruction booklet recipes to see the typical flour to liquid ratio for your machine.

Poppy Seed Rolls

These yummy little rolls are perfect for tea with butter and a really good jam but they are also great for breakfast, packed lunches or to serve with soup. The beaten egg gives a shiny golden finish and the poppy seeds, which stay on surprisingly well, have a nice nutty crunch.

You can buy special poppy seeds for baking: they are usually sold in the spice section of supermarkets and these are from the Hungarian Blue Breadseed Poppy. This is a variety of the opium poppy *Papaver somniferum*, and the seeds have a distinctive beautiful blue sheen.

Makes 12 rolls

For the rolls

300ml warm skimmed milk	1 tablespoon sugar
2 tablespoons mild oil	400g strong white bread flour
1 teaspoon salt	1 teaspoon quick yeast

For the glaze and topping

1 egg, beaten with a drop of water   About 2 dessertspoons of poppy seeds

You will need a large greased baking tray

1. Pour the milk and oil into the bread pan of your machine and add the salt and sugar, placing them at different ends of the pan. Put the flour on top and finally the yeast. Select the **Basic Dough** programme.

2. Once the dough is ready, take it out of the machine and flour your hands well before removing it from the bread pan. Put the dough onto a floured surface and knead it for a few moments.

3. Divide it into four pieces and divide each of those into a further three pieces. Roll each of these pieces into a long cylindrical tube about 30cm long.

4. You can make at least four different shapes from the long cylinders. Here are the main ones but you may come up with others:

Plait Plait three of the pieces together and cut the plait into three equal pieces;

Twist Twist two of the pieces together and cut the twist into three equal pieces;

Coil Cut a long cylinder into three sections and coil each section round on itself so that it looks a bit like a snail shell;

Knot Cut a long cylinder into three sections and tie each section carefully into a knot.

5. Put the finished shapes onto the prepared baking tray and leave in a warm place for about an hour until they have almost doubled in size and look about the right size for the finished rolls.

6. Once they are at this stage, brush them carefully with the beaten egg and sprinkle with the poppy seeds.

7. Bake in a preheated oven at 180-220°C (fan ovens) or equivalent for 8-10 minutes until the tops are golden.

8. Cool on a wire rack: a clean tea towel laid over the rolls will keep them moist as they cool.

If the flour to liquid ratio doesn't seem quite right for your machine, in that the amount of liquid seems too great, try increasing the total flour measurement to 500g and decrease the milk to 260ml. Check with your machine's instruction booklet recipes to see the typical flour to liquid ratio for your machine.

Muffins

(Oven-baked)

Traditional English muffins are usually cooked on a griddle but in this simple recipe they are baked in the oven, which is fuss-free and reliable. A second baking tray placed on top of the muffins as they bake will give the characteristic flat tops.

Muffins are a lovely nostalgic treat for a cosy winter teatime. You can eat them split and spread with soft butter while they are still fresh and warm or leave them to cool and eat them later split and lightly toasted.

A toasted muffin is the perfect partner for a poached egg or two. You can make a great weekend breakfast with fried egg and bacon sandwiched in a lightly toasted muffin. For the more delicate Egg Benedict, poach the egg, change the bacon for wafer thin ham, and add a spoonful of hollandaise sauce: alternatively, make an even more luxurious version with smoked salmon instead of ham.

Makes 6

180ml slightly warm skimmed milk	1 teaspoon sugar
2 tablespoons mild oil	300g strong white bread flour
1 teaspoon salt	½ teaspoon quick yeast

A little ground rice for dusting

You will need 2 baking trays and a 9cm straight-sided cutter

1. Pour the milk and oil into the bread pan of your machine with the salt and sugar, placing them at different ends of the bread pan. Put the flour on top and add the yeast. Select the **Basic Dough** programme.

2. Once the dough is ready, remove it from the machine with lightly floured hands and put it onto a lightly floured board.

3. Using a lightly floured rolling pin, roll the dough gently to a thickness of about a centimetre and cut out 6 rounds.

4. Grease one of the baking trays and space out the muffins upon it. Leave them to prove in a warm spot until they have almost doubled in size.

5. Preheat your oven to your usual bread-baking temperature of 180–220°C (fan oven) or equivalent.

6. Dust the muffins with ground rice for a professional-looking finish; stir it through a tea strainer for a nice even distribution.

7. Grease the bottom of the second tray and place on top of the muffins. Put the two trays into the oven together and bake the muffins for approximately 10 minutes until they are a light golden brown.

8. Cool on a wire rack, covered with a clean tea towel to keep them fresh and moist.

This receipe is suitable for most types of bread machine.

Simple Rustic Loaf

This loaf is a bit like the Italian focaccia and is simplicity itself to make. It's lovely fresh from the oven, perfect for a simple bread and cheese lunch or with soup, and it makes great garlic bread. It's also very easy to fancy it up impressively with a few strategically placed holes or dimples, rosemary and sea salt; see below for some suggestions.

180ml warm water	1 teaspoon salt
2 tablespoons olive oil, plus more for the top	300g strong white bread flour
	½ teaspoon quick yeast

You will need a large greased baking tray

1. Pour the water and oil into the bread pan of your machine with the salt. Put the flour on top and add the yeast. Select the **Basic Dough** programme.

2. Once the dough is ready, remove it from the machine with lightly floured hands and knead it briefly on a lightly floured work surface.

3. Mould it into a round. Use one hand and roll it round your work surface until you get the right flattish bun shape.

4. Ease it onto the prepared baking tray and leave to prove until it has almost doubled in size.

5. Preheat your oven to your usual bread-baking temperature of 180-220°C (fan oven) or equivalent. Just before you put the loaf in the oven, drizzle with olive oil and spread the oil completely over the surface.

6. Bake for 18-20 minutes until golden.

Optional dimples, salt and rosemary
You may wish to perk up the appearance of your loaf a bit with a few random dimples using your fingertips (not advisable if you have nails of any length), or make a few smaller, neater holes using something like a clean seed dibber. Do this before you drizzle the oil over the top. You could also sprinkle the loaf with flakes of sea salt and tuck in tiny sprigs of rosemary.

If the flour to liquid ratio doesn't seem quite right for your machine, in that the amount of liquid seems too great, try increasing the total flour measurement to 350g. Check with your machine's instruction booklet recipes to see the typical flour to liquid ratio for your machine.

Cheese Bread

This is lovely eaten still warm, fresh from the oven. It's good with soup and tomato-based pasta dishes and great to pack for a picnic. If you're not going far, and you have time to bake before you set off, you can wrap the loaf in a tea towel and keep it warm until you arrive at your destination. The mustard powder helps to bring out the flavour of the cheese but leave it out if you prefer.

As well as flavouring the bread, the cheese makes the dough very smooth and silky – and the finished texture of the loaf very soft. The bread will rise higher during baking.

If you would like an even cheesier flavour, use a stronger vintage cheese, but keep to the amount specified in the recipe; adding more cheese will alter the texture of the bread and make it too heavy, particularly in the centre.

260ml warm water	400g strong white bread flour
100g mature Cheddar cheese, grated, plus more for top (optional)	1 teaspoon mustard powder (optional)
	1 teaspoon quick yeast
½ teaspoon salt	
1 tablespoon sugar	Extra grated cheese for topping (optional)

You will need a large greased baking tray

1. Sieve the mustard powder (a tea strainer is handy for this) over the flour as you weigh the flour on the scales.

2. Pour the water into the bread pan of your machine and add the cheese. Add the salt and sugar, placing them at separate ends of the bread pan. Put the flour and mustard on top and add the yeast. Select the **Dough** programme

3. Once the dough is ready, remove it from the machine with lightly floured hands and knead it briefly on a lightly floured work surface.

4. Mould it into a round. Use one hand and roll it round your work surface until you get the right flattish bun shape.

5. Ease it onto the prepared baking tray and leave to prove until it has almost doubled in size.

6. Preheat your oven to your usual bread-baking temperature of 180–220°C (fan oven) or equivalent.

7. If you wish, just before you put the loaf in the oven, grate a little cheese over the top: not too much, just a small amount across the centre. It's a good idea to do this if you have guests and are serving more than one kind of bread as it helps to distinguish the cheese bread from the others.

8. Bake for 25–30 minutes until golden.

Note: The cheese content in this recipe makes the mixture extra rich, or 'short', which means it tends to perform successfully in most types of machine without altering the original amounts of flour and liquid in the mixture.

Cheese Toast – with or without Marmite

The cheese bread will keep fresh and moist for a good couple of days and after that it makes fantastic toast. Eat it plain with butter or add a light scraping of Marmite.

Toasted cheese bread also adds a new dimension to baked beans on toast.

Walnut Bread

Bake this plump and generous loaf to cut at over the weekend or for when you have guests.

Walnut bread is delicious cut into chunks and either simply buttered or served with cheese. It goes particularly well with soft and blue cheeses or autumnal preserves such as plum jam or quince jelly. Slice it more thinly to make delicious sandwiches with Brie and a little redcurrant or cranberry jelly.

Once it's a day or two old, try it thickly sliced and lightly toasted. It makes a perfect light Sunday supper with some blue cheese, a bit of salad and perhaps a heartening glass of red wine.

Half the walnuts are added at the beginning, to become incorporated into the dough for maximum flavour, and the rest later so that they remain whole for texture and interest.

300ml warm water	50g chopped walnuts
2 tablespoons mild oil	1 teaspoon quick yeast
1 teaspoon salt	
1 tablespoon sugar	
300g strong white bread flour	Additional 50g chopped walnuts
100g strong wholemeal bread flour	A little more oil for the top

You will need a large greased baking tray

1. Pour the water and oil into the bread pan of your machine and add the salt and sugar, placing them at different ends of the pan. Put the flours on top with 50g of chopped walnuts and add the yeast.

2. Select the **Basic Dough** programme with **Raisin** option – either put the remaining 50g walnuts in the raisin compartment, if your machine has one, or set the raisin beep and add them when it sounds.

3. Once the dough is ready, remove it from the machine with lightly floured hands and knead it briefly on a lightly floured work surface.

4. Mould it into a round. Use one hand and roll it round your work surface until you get the right flattish bun shape.

5. Ease it onto the prepared baking tray and leave to prove until it has almost doubled in size.

6. Preheat your oven to your usual bread-baking temperature of 180–220°C (fan oven) or equivalent.

7. Just before you put the loaf in the oven, drizzle with oil and spread the oil completely over the surface; you can do this most easily with your fingers.

8. Bake for 40–45 minutes until golden brown. If you are unsure whether the loaf is baked right through, take it out of the oven and tap the bottom: it should sound hollow.

If you have no raisin option, knead the second lot of walnuts into the dough once it is ready and you have taken it out of the machine.

If the flour to liquid ratio doesn't seem quite right for your machine, in that the amount of liquid seems too great, try increasing the total flour measurement to 500g and decrease the water to 260ml. Check with your machine's instruction booklet recipes to see the typical flour to liquid ratio for your machine.

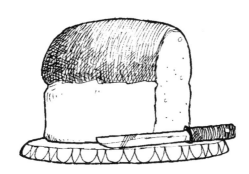

Olive Bread

This goes well with Italian-style dishes or cheese and some fresh salad. If you are entertaining, and have the time, a selection of Olive Bread, Cheese Bread and Simple Rustic Loaf works well.

300ml warm water	400g strong white bread flour
2 tablespoons olive oil, plus more for top	1 teaspoon quick yeast
1 teaspoon salt	
1 tablespoon sugar	50g pitted black olives

You will need a large greased baking tray

1. Pat the olives dry of any brine and cut each olive into quarters or chop roughly. Leave on kitchen paper to drain further.

2. Pour the water and olive oil into the bread pan of your machine and add the salt and sugar, placing them at different ends of the pan. Put the flour on top and add the yeast.

3. Select the **Basic Dough** programme with **Raisin** option – either put the olives in the raisin compartment, if your machine has one, or set the raisin beep and add the olives when it sounds.

4. Once the dough is ready, remove it from the machine with lightly floured hands and knead it briefly on a lightly floured work surface.

5. Mould it into a round. Use one hand and roll it round your work surface until you get the right flattish bun shape.

6. Ease it onto the prepared baking tray and leave to prove until it has almost doubled in size.

7. Preheat your oven to your usual bread-baking temperature of 180–220°C (fan oven) or equivalent.

8. Just before you put the loaf in the oven, drizzle with olive oil and spread the oil completely over the surface; you can do this most easily with your fingers.

9. Bake for 18–20 minutes until golden.

10. Transfer to a wire rack to cool.

If you have no raisin option, knead the olives into the dough once it is ready and you have taken it out of the machine.

If the flour to liquid ratio doesn't seem quite right for your machine, in that the amount of liquid seems too great, try increasing the total flour measurement to 500g and decrease the water to 260ml. Check with your machine's instruction booklet recipes to see the typical flour to liquid ratio for your machine.

USING WHAT'S TO HAND TO ENHANCE YOUR LOAVES

It used to be said of Cornish wives that they could turn anything into a pasty. Apparently, so the story goes, Satan was reluctant to stand anywhere for very long in that county for fear of being put into a pasty himself.

It can get a bit like that once you start making bread: you can use ingredients you happen to have to hand to enhance your loaves, giving them a slightly different and appealing taste and texture.

Intriguingly, ingredients you would expect to impart a sweet flavour to the bread, such as banana and apple, don't necessarily, but simply add a subtle background flavour with extra moistness or a slight chewiness.

Courgette Loaf

If courgettes are running amok in your vegetable plot during the summer, here is an unusual way to utilise them. You may well be asking yourself why on earth you would want to put courgette in bread. Admittedly, it seems a bit eccentric but the courgette gives an extra lightness and moisture to the loaf and you will notice it rises higher than normal. The courgette also imparts a subtle sweet flavour and extends the loaf's keeping qualities. If you look closely at the cut surface, you will notice small, intriguing green flecks but you won't actually be able to taste courgette.

If seeds have begun to form, cut the courgettes lengthways and use a teaspoon to scrape out the seedy bits.

160ml warm water	1 tablespoon sugar
2 tablespoons mild oil	400g strong white bread flour
100g courgette, peeled and grated	1 teaspoon quick yeast
1 teaspoon salt	

You will need a greased baking tray

1. Pour the water and oil into the bread pan of your machine and add the courgette. Place the salt and sugar at different ends of the pan. Add the flour and put the yeast centrally on top. Select the **Basic Dough** programme.

2. Once the dough is ready, remove it from the machine with lightly floured hands and knead it briefly on a lightly floured work surface.

3. Mould it into a round. Use one hand and roll it round your work surface until you get the right flattish bun shape. Ease it onto the prepared baking tray and leave to prove until it has almost doubled in size.

4. Preheat your oven to your usual bread-baking temperature of 180–220°C (fan oven) or equivalent and bake for around 30 minutes until golden brown.

5. Leave to settle and contract away from the sides of the tin for a few minutes and then transfer to a wire rack to cool.

This recipe is suitable for most types of bread machine.

Spreadable Butter

Many of us would agree that the flavour of pure butter complements your home-baked bread much better than any vegetable-based spread. However, some of the soft spreadable butters that have only a little oil added to actual butter are very good and very easy to use. It's simple to make your own spreadable butter at home in a food processor. All you need is some softened butter and a little mild oil: sunflower and rapeseed both work well.

140g softened butter
60ml mild, flavourless oil such as rapeseed or sunflower

1. Put the softened butter into the bowl of the food processor and give it a quick whizz. Add 3-4 teaspoons of the oil and whizz to incorporate. Scrape the mixture down from the sides with a flexible spatula and add the rest of the oil gradually, whizzing in 3-4 teaspoons at a time.

2. Transfer to a covered container and store in the fridge. The plastic tubs that commercial spreadable butter comes in are ideal for storage.

3. If you feel this is too much oil and not enough butter, reduce the oil to 40-50ml. Experiment until you achieve your preferred combination.

Banana Bread

Banana bread isn't sweet as such. It's more that the banana adds a certain moistness and chewiness with a subtle flavour you can't quite put your finger on.

As well as buttered at teatime or for breakfast, banana bread is especially good for certain sandwiches, notably honey, peanut butter, banana or cream cheese. Less predictably, banana bread makes a fine ham sandwich. Banana bread also makes delicious breakfast toast once it is a day or two old.

Use bananas that are ripe but not *completely* overripe: the skin may be starting to speckle but the flesh should still be creamy white and not soft and brown.

175g banana, peeled weight (don't add more than this, just to 'use it up', or the bread will be heavy)	2 tablespoons mild oil
	1 teaspoon salt
	1 tablespoon sugar
	400g strong white bread flour
160ml warm water	1 teaspoon quick yeast

You will need a greased 450g loaf tin

1. Mash the banana until smooth but not liquidy.

2. Pour the water and oil into the bread pan of your machine and add the salt and sugar, placing them at different ends of the pan. Put the flour on top.

3. Add the mashed banana, and finally the yeast, positioning it on top of the flour and clear of the banana. Select the **Basic Dough** programme.

4. Once the dough is ready, remove it from the machine with lightly floured hands and knead it briefly on a lightly floured work surface.

5. Mould it into an approximate oval shape and put it into the prepared loaf tin. Leave to prove until almost doubled in size.

6. Preheat your oven to your usual bread-baking temperature of 180–220°C (fan oven) or equivalent and bake for around 30 minutes until golden brown.

7. Leave to settle and contract away from the sides of the tin for a few minutes and then transfer to a wire rack to cool.

This recipe is suitable for most types of bread machine.

Banana Bread with Wholemeal or Malted Granary Flour

Prepare the dough as for the main recipe but swap 100g of the white flour for wholemeal or malted granary flour.

Apple Bread

The grated apple makes this loaf beautifully moist with a slight chewiness. It imparts an especially fresh, sweet smell and gives it quite a spectacular rise. It doesn't taste of apples as such but there is something elusive there in the background. This loaf is particularly good with cheese or ham. It keeps well and makes wonderful toast after the first couple of days.

160ml warm water	400g strong white bread flour
2 tablespoons mild oil	175g grated apple
1 teaspoon salt	1 teaspoon quick yeast
1 tablespoon sugar	

You will need a greased 450g loaf tin

1. Pour the water and oil into the bread pan of your machine and add the salt and sugar. Put the flour on top.

2. Add the grated apple, and finally the yeast, positioning it on top of the flour and clear of the apple. Select the **Basic Dough** programme.

3. Once the dough is ready, remove it from the machine with lightly floured hands and knead it briefly on a lightly floured work surface.

4. Mould it into an approximate oval shape and put it into the prepared loaf tin. Leave to prove until almost doubled in size.

5. Preheat your oven to your usual bread-baking temperature of 180–220°C (fan oven) or equivalent and bake for around 30 minutes until golden brown.

6. Leave to settle and contract away from the sides of the tin for a few minutes and then transfer to a wire rack to cool.

This recipe is suitable for most types of bread machine.

Apple Bread with Wholemeal Flour

Prepare the dough as for the main recipe but swap 100g of the white flour for wholemeal flour.

Wholemeal Apple Bread

The freshness and moistness of the apple combines well with the nutty flavour of the wholemeal flour.

170ml warm water

2 tablespoons mild oil

1 teaspoon salt

1 tablespoon sugar

400g strong wholemeal bread flour

175g grated apple

1 teaspoon quick yeast

You will need a large greased baking tray

1. Pour the water and oil into the bread pan of your machine and add the salt and sugar. Put the flour on top.

2. Add the grated apple, and finally the yeast, positioning it on top of the flour and clear of the apple. Select the **Whole wheat Dough** programme.

3. Once the dough is ready, remove it from the machine with lightly floured hands and knead it briefly on a lightly floured work surface.

4. Mould it into a round. Use one hand and roll it round your work surface until you get the right flattish bun shape.

5. Ease it onto the prepared baking tray and leave to prove until it has almost doubled in size.

6. Preheat your oven to your usual bread-baking temperature of 180–220°C (fan oven) or equivalent and bake for around 30 minutes until golden brown.

7. Transfer to a wire rack to cool.

This recipe is suitable for most types of bread machine.

Potato Bread

Potato bread has a lovely moist fluffiness; it keeps well and is a great way to use up any leftover mashed or boiled potatoes. If you can manage to save some cooking water from your potatoes, use that for the bread as well. In fact, potato cooking water is always worth using to make your bread with as the starch it contains will give any loaf an extra rise.

Once potato bread is a day or two old, it makes fantastic toast.

....

100g cold cooked potatoes, mashed   1 teaspoon salt
    or boiled   1 tablespoon sugar
150ml water, use potato cooking   400g strong white bread flour
    water, if available   1 teaspoon quick yeast
2 tablespoons mild oil

....

You will need a greased 450g loaf tin or a greased baking tray

1. If the potatoes aren't already mashed, mash them with a fork.

2. Pour the water and oil into the bread pan of your machine and add the salt and sugar, placing them at different ends of the pan. Put the flour on top.

3. Add the mashed potato, and finally the yeast, positioning it on top of the flour and clear of the potato. Select the **Basic Dough** programme.

4. Once the dough is ready, remove it from the machine with lightly floured hands and knead it briefly on a floured board.

5. Mould it into an approximate oval shape and put it into the prepared loaf tin or mould it into a round and put it onto the prepared tray. Leave to prove until almost doubled in size.

6. Preheat your oven to your usual bread-baking temperature of 180-220°C (fan oven) or equivalent and bake for around 25–30 minutes until golden.

7. Transfer to a wire rack to cool. If you have baked the loaf in a tin, allow a few moments for it to contract away from the sides of the tin before cooling on the rack.

Note: If you are using leftover potato mashed with vast amounts of butter and cream the bread may turn out a little on the heavy side.

This recipe is suitable for most types of bread machine.

Potato Bread Farls

The shape of these is based on potato farls, potato cakes made from leftover mashed potato and a little flour, which are fried as part of a traditional Ulster Fry – the popular cooked breakfast served in Northern Ireland. A farl is a round cut into four quarters, from the Gaelic for four parts.

These potato bread farls are fluffy and moist and are fantastic split and spread with a little butter: try serving them with bacon and eggs.

Makes 8 farls

100g cold cooked potatoes, mashed or boiled	1 teaspoon salt
	1 tablespoon sugar
150ml water, use potato cooking water, if available	400g strong white bread flour
	1 teaspoon quick yeast
1 tablespoon mild oil	

You will need a large greased baking tray

1. If the potatoes aren't already mashed, mash them with a fork.

2. Pour the water and oil into the bread pan of your machine and add the salt and sugar. Put the flour on top.

3. Add the mashed potato, and finally the yeast, positioning it on top of the flour and clear of the potato. Select the **Basic Dough** programme.

4. Once the dough is ready transfer it with floured hands to a lightly floured board. Knead it briefly and divide it into two: it's a good idea to weigh the pieces.

5. Mould each piece into a round and flatten into a disc about the size of a tea plate. You can do this with your hands but a lightly floured rolling pin is helpful. Transfer the discs to the prepared baking tray.

6. Leave them in a warm place until they have almost doubled in size. Mark both pieces into quarters or farls with a biggish sharp knife that has a non-serrated blade. Don't cut all the way through the dough but make sure the quarters are clearly defined.

7. Bake in a preheated oven at 220°C (fan oven) or equivalent for 20–25 minutes until golden and cooked through.

8. For a nice final extra touch dust the potato farls with flour; stir it through a tea strainer for light, even distribution.

This recipe is suitable for most types of bread machine.

Rice Bread

This is an interesting loaf to make, not unlike potato bread in texture as the extra starch in the rice gives the same light fluffiness. It's a handy and novel way to use leftover rice and works best of all with well-cooked rice; if you like your rice too 'al dente' it will tend to stay in separate grains and not be incorporated into the dough so well. Plus, the rice needs to contain a certain amount of moisture to enhance the bread.

A word of warning: whilst the inside of the loaf is beautifully soft and moist and the rice is absorbed well into the dough (see above), there may be a few rogue whole grains of rice lurking in the crust which can be a bit on the crunchy side! As with potato bread, rice bread makes excellent toast after a couple of days.

Cool the leftover rice quickly after it has been cooked initially and refrigerate until you are ready to make your bread. Use the rice within 24 hours.

100g cold boiled rice	1 tablespoon sugar
260ml water	400g strong white bread flour
1 tablespoon mild oil	1 teaspoon quick yeast
1 teaspoon salt	

You will need a greased 450g loaf tin or a greased baking tray

1. Fluff up and separate the rice if it is sticking together.

2. Pour the water and oil into the bread pan of your machine and add the salt and sugar followed by the rice. Put the flour on top and finally the yeast. Select the **Basic Dough** programme.

3. Once the dough is ready, remove it from the machine with lightly floured hands and knead it briefly on a floured board.

4. Mould it into an oval shape and put it into the prepared loaf tin, or mould it into a round and put it onto the prepared tray. Leave to prove until almost doubled in size.

5. Preheat your oven to your usual bread-baking temperature of 180-220°C (fan oven) or equivalent. Bake for around 30 minutes until golden brown.

6. Transfer to a wire rack to cool – if you have baked the loaf in a tin, allow a few moments for it to contract away from the sides of the tin before cooling on the rack.

Helpful note: If you only have a couple of spoonfuls or so of well-cooked rice left over – say 50–75g – try including it in any of the white bread loaf or roll recipes for a bit of added fluffiness.

This recipe is suitable for most types of bread machine.

Beer Bread

Who first discovered that yeast made bread rise, and how? We will probably never know for sure, but one theory is that, initially, people may have used ale instead of water to mix their dough, noticed the lighter result and investigated further. Certainly, generations ago people would use leaven or yeast from the local brewery.

This modern version with added sugar, yeast and oil, makes a loaf with a beautiful soft, fine texture and an elusive ale-like flavour. It's a good all-purpose loaf and goes particularly well with sausages and mustard. It's also good toasted and spread with a little Marmite; the beery, yeasty flavours complement each other nicely.

Use beer at room temperature, rather than from the fridge. If you make this often, you can play about with the beer and water ratios depending on how strong an ale flavour you like.

200ml strong real ale: home brew can work well	1 teaspoon salt
	1 tablespoon sugar
100ml water	400g strong white bread flour
2 tablespoons mild oil	1 teaspoon quick yeast

You will need a greased baking tray

1. Hold your measuring cup at an angle and pour the ale gently down the side. Leave to settle while you assemble the rest of the ingredients.

2. Pour the ale into the bread pan of your machine with the water and oil and add the salt and sugar. Put the flour on top and finally add the yeast. Select the **Basic Dough** programme.

3. Once the dough is ready, remove it from the machine with lightly floured hands and knead it briefly on a floured board.

4. Mould it into a round. Use one hand and roll it round your work surface until you get the right flattish bun shape.

5. Ease it onto the prepared baking tray and leave to prove until it has almost doubled in size.

6. Preheat your oven to your usual bread-baking temperature of 180–220°C (fan oven) or equivalent. Bake for around 25–30 minutes until golden brown. Alternatively, bake the bread in a greased 450g loaf tin for 25–30 minutes.

7. Transfer to a wire rack to cool. Cheers!

If the flour to liquid ratio doesn't seem quite right for your machine, in that the amount of liquid seems too great, try increasing the total flour measurement to 500g and decrease the total liquid to 260ml. Check with your machine's instruction booklet recipes to see the typical flour to liquid ratio for your machine.

Cider Bread

Continuing with the brewing theme, here is a loaf made with cider. It's interesting to compare the two as the flavour is quite different but the texture is similar. The cider should be of the still variety: nothing gassy or fizzy. Cider bread makes an excellent ploughman's lunch.

300ml still cider	1 tablespoon sugar
2 tablespoons mild oil	400g strong white bread flour
1 teaspoon salt	1 teaspoon quick yeast

You will need a greased baking tray

1. Pour the cider into the bread pan of your machine with the oil and add the salt and sugar. Put the flour on top and finally add the yeast. Select the **Basic Dough** programme.

2. Once the dough is ready, remove it from the machine with lightly floured hands and knead it briefly on a floured board.

3. Mould it into a round. Use one hand and roll it round your work surface until you get the right flattish bun shape.

4. Ease it onto the prepared baking tray and leave to prove until it has almost doubled in size.

5. Preheat your oven to your usual bread-baking temperature of 180–220°C (fan oven) or equivalent. Bake for around 25–30 minutes until golden brown. Alternatively, bake the bread in a greased 450g loaf tin for 25–30 minutes.

6. Transfer to a wire rack to cool.

If the flour to liquid ratio doesn't seem quite right for your machine, in that the amount of liquid seems too great, try increasing the total flour measurement to 500g and decrease the total liquid to 260ml. Check with your machine's instruction booklet recipes to see the typical flour to liquid ratio for your machine.

TAKING CARE OF YOUR BREAD MACHINE

Wipe the outside of the actual machine regularly with a damp cloth and a little mild detergent. Pay particular attention to around the lid area.

The bread pan tends to stay quite clean with loaves made entirely in the machine but dough can sometimes stick to the inside of the bread pan slightly.

Sometimes all the pan needs is a wipe with a damp cloth or sometimes it needs to be filled with warm water and some washing up liquid and allowed to soak for a while. Obviously, never immerse the whole pan in water.

Wash and soak the mixing blade regularly. Sometimes dough can become stuck in the spindle hole so remove with a wooden cocktail stick: never use anything metal.

If traces of dough become stuck to the side of the pan, allow the dough to dry out so you can brush it away before you soak it.

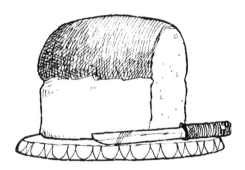

Lavender and Honey Bread

The lavender makes this quite an unusual loaf that tastes wonderful. The lavender flavour is very gentle but you can tell it is there. The honey flavour comes through subtly as well. This is great for a relaxed meal in the garden: serve with a little butter, thin slices of cheese and a green salad. It's also delicious buttered and spread with a creamy set honey or a good jam or jelly: bramble or crab apple jelly is especially nice. Lavender bread is also good toasted, spread with butter and honey for breakfast: the lavender scent really comes through as it warms up in the toaster.

A word of warning: be sure to use only the more common English lavender, Lavandula *angustifolia*, sometimes called Lavendula *officinalis* or Lavandula *spicata*. The tufty French lavender, Lavandula *stoechas*, can be toxic.

300ml warm water
2 tablespoons mild oil
1 teaspoon salt
1 tablespoon runny honey

400g strong white bread flour
1 teaspoon quick yeast
15–20 sprigs of lavender flowers still in bud

You will need a greased 450g loaf tin or a greased baking tray

1. Lay the lavender sprigs on kitchen paper for a while to dry out and allow any small creatures (if there are any) to leave. Remove all the florets from the stalks and shake them lightly in a sieve.

2. Pour the water and oil into the bread pan of your machine and add the salt and honey. Put the flour on top and finally add the yeast.

3. Select the **Dough** programme with **Raisin** option – either put the lavender in the raisin compartment, if your machine has one, or wait for or set the raisin beep and add it when it sounds.

4. Once the dough is ready, remove it from the machine with lightly floured hands and knead it briefly on a floured board.

5. Mould it into an approximate oval shape and put it into the prepared loaf tin or mould it into a round and put it onto the prepared tray. Leave to prove until almost doubled in size.

6. Preheat your oven to your usual bread-baking temperature of 180-220°C (fan oven) or equivalent. Bake for around 30 minutes until golden brown.

7. Transfer to a wire rack to cool – if you have baked the loaf in a tin, allow a few moments for it to contract away from the sides of the tin before cooling on the rack.

If you have no raisin option, knead the lavender into the dough once it is ready and you have taken it out of the machine.

If the flour to liquid ratio doesn't seem quite right for your machine, in that the amount of liquid seems too great, try increasing the total flour measurement to 500g and decrease the water to 260ml. Check with your machine's instruction booklet recipes to see the typical flour to liquid ratio for your machine.

Staffordshire Oatcakes

These are not most people's idea of oatcakes: instead of the expected hard biscuit-type cake they are more like an oaty pancake. Although attributed to Staffordshire, they are also popular in Derbyshire and are available throughout both counties from shops, cafes and takeaways. People who move away from Staffordshire and Derbyshire often miss them enormously and buy as many as they can to take home when they return for a visit.

They can be eaten either hot or cold, with bacon and eggs or wrapped round sausages for breakfast, or with butter and jam or honey at teatime. Sausage and cheese is another popular combination. Staffordshire oatcakes are really popular with children for breakfast with honey.

You can easily make the batter in a bowl, but since you have your bread machine standing by, it makes sense to put it to good use to whip up a decent fuss-free batch of oatcakes. Be prepared for some interesting sloshing and glooping noises issuing from your machine.

This recipe uses semi-skimmed milk, but you can use half whole milk, half water, as is more traditional, if you prefer.

Note: Use ordinary plain flour for this recipe.

Makes 6-8

450ml semi-skimmed milk	125g plain flour
½ teaspoon sugar	125g fine oatmeal
½ teaspoon salt	2 teaspoons quick yeast

Melted butter or oil for frying

You will need a medium frying pan, approximately 20-23cm in diameter

1. Put the milk, sugar and salt in the bread pan, and the flour, oatmeal and yeast on top. Select the **Dough** programme.

2. Run the programme for 20-30 minutes until the batter is fully mixed and then switch off. You may need to hold the switch down for several seconds before it engages.

3. Once it is ready, pour the batter into a jug with a good pouring spout and set aside.

4. Brush your frying pan with melted butter or oil and put on the hob over a medium-hot temperature.

5. When the pan is hot, pour in a couple of tablespoons of batter, enough to cover the bottom.

6. Cook the oatcake for 2 or 3 minutes and, once the edges are lifting slightly, turn it over and cook the other side.

7. Eat immediately or pile the oatcakes on a plate and keep warm, covered with a clean tea towel to prevent them drying out, until you have cooked the whole batch.

Half Plain, Half Wholemeal Staffordshire Oatcakes

You can also make these oatcakes using 65g each of plain and wholemeal flour.

Staffordshire Oatcakes with Sausage and Cheese Filling

A popular Staffordshire oatcake filling is sausage and melted cheese. Instead of using grated cheese on its own, make a thick cheese sauce with milk and cornflour. This is smoother and less heavy than plain melted cheese and tastes fine cold, unlike cold melted cheese which can be a bit rubbery and congealed.

150ml milk, whole or semi-skimmed
150g well-flavoured Cheddar cheese, grated

2 level tablespoons cornflour (use the tablespoon measure that comes with your bread machine)

You will need a small, heavy-bottomed milk pan (you can mix the milk and cornflour in the pan, off the heat, to save washing up)

1. Mix the cornflour to a smooth paste with a little of the cold milk and gradually stir in the rest.

2. Put the pan over a moderate heat and stir until the mixture thickens. Add the grated cheese and stir until it has all melted.

3. Spread some of the filling onto your oatcake, place a hot sausage on top and roll up.

Staffordshire Oatcakes with Plain Cheese and Cheese and Bacon Fillings

You can also spread your oatcake with the cheese filling on its own or with a combination of cheese filling and a rasher of freshly fried or grilled bacon.

Leftover cheese filling
If you have any cheese filling left over, it makes a great toasted cheese sandwich. You can store it, covered, in the fridge for the best part of a week. It will spread easily straight from the fridge.

Easy Pancake Batter

Obviously, you can easily make pancake batter in a bowl, but it's just so simple to put all the ingredients in the bread machine and let it get on with it. As with the Staffordshire Oatcakes, be prepared to hear some interesting sloshing noises coming from the bread machine.

Note: Use ordinary plain flour for this recipe.

570ml semi-skimmed milk

2 medium eggs, lightly beaten

Pinch of salt

225g plain flour

Butter and/or oil (melted butter gives the best flavour) for frying

You will need a medium frying pan approximately 20–23cm in diameter

1. Put the milk, eggs and salt in the bread pan, and the flour on top. Select the **Pizza Dough** programme – or the shortest dough programme for your machine.

2. Run the programme for roughly 20 minutes until the batter is fully mixed and then switch off. You may need to hold the switch down for several seconds before it engages.

3. Once it is ready, pour the batter into a jug with a good pouring spout and set aside.

4. Brush the pan with melted butter, or oil, if you prefer. Put the pan on to heat, on a medium to high setting, and get it really hot.

5. Pour the batter into the middle of the pan, until you have covered an area about the size of a large fried egg, and flick the pan in a circular motion until the batter spreads to cover the whole of the pan.

6. Cook the pancake for a couple of minutes until it will move freely in the pan when you shake it. Flip it over with a fish slice and cook for another couple of minutes until you can shake the pan as before.

Flour Tortillas

It's very handy to be able to whip up a batch of tortillas at home, and although you can mix the dough by hand, it seems much easier just to pop it in your bread machine and turn on the **Pizza Dough** programme - or the shortest dough programme for your machine.

These tortillas are 'flour tortillas', made with wheat flour, as distinct from the corn tortillas made from maize meal. Flour tortillas used to be more prevalent in northern Mexico where maize was rarely grown and are much less specialised to make than corn ones.

Fill with savoury Mexican-inspired dishes, or anything you want to make into a wrap, and roll up or fold into quarters or pockets. Although absolutely not authentic at all, these are also good to wrap round Peking duck with hoisin sauce, spring onions and matchsticks of cucumber.

These are also popular with children, spread with butter and honey or sugar and rolled into a cylinder.

Note: Use ordinary plain flour for this recipe.

Makes around 10

140ml warm water	40g lard or vegetable shortening, diced
½ teaspoon salt	225g plain flour, plus more for rolling
Melted butter or oil for frying	

You will need a medium frying pan approximately 20-23cm in diameter

1. Put all the water, salt and lard or vegetable shortening into the bread pan and the flour on top. Select the **Pizza Dough** programme - or the shortest dough programme for your machine.

2. Run the programme for 20-30 minutes until the dough has formed into a smooth, compact ball and then switch off. You may need to hold the switch down for several seconds before it engages.

3. Once the dough is ready, transfer it to a lightly floured board and divide into 10 equal pieces.

4. Knead each piece in your hands and fold it over a couple of times and flatten it to knock out some of the air.

5. Form into a ball and, using a floured rolling pin, roll into a wafer-thin pancake shape. Don't stint on the flour for rolling as the finished tortilla should be faintly floury in appearance.

6. You can fry these just as they are or, alternatively, for a neat, round, professional-looking tortilla, invert a small plate on top of the rolled out dough and cut round it with the point of a knife. Remove the trimmings before you lift away the plate as the tortillas can very easily tear and become misshapen.

7. Brush your frying pan with melted butter or oil and place on the hob over a medium-hot heat.

8. Transfer each tortilla in the flat of your hand and manoeuvre it carefully into the pan: try to get it perfectly flat with no creases. There is a bit of an art to this but it doesn't take long to become proficient.

9. Cook each tortilla for a couple of minutes or so on each side, turning it over once you see the characteristic 'bubbles' forming and the tortilla seems to be thickening slightly. Don't overcook: they should be soft and pliable, and not at all stiff.

10. Eat immediately or pile the tortillas on a plate and keep them warm, covered with a clean tea towel to prevent them from drying out, until you have cooked the whole batch. Eat while still fresh and warm.

Hybrid Tortillas with Fine Cornmeal

These are simply soft wheat tortillas made with a combination of white wheat flour and fine cornmeal. They are delicious but not to be confused with corn tortillas, which are a slightly more complicated recipe resulting in a different kind of firm tortilla – the type that taco shells are made from.

Make as for the main recipe but swap 100g of the white flour for fine cornmeal and use more fine cornmeal for rolling out.

These are fabulous wrapped around a spicy butcher's sausage: preferably one seasoned with fiery chillies.

Pitta Bread

It's much easier than you might think to make pitta bread. The baking time is very short and it's fun to watch them puff up in the oven. Once you've got the hang of it, you can make wholemeal pittas and mini party pittas as well. They are best served fresh from the oven while they are still warm. If you are eating them cold keep them covered with a clean tea towel as they cool to prevent them from drying out. Cut the pittas in half and open them out, or make a little slit in the top of each pitta and insert the filling of your choice. Alternatively, cut them into strips to serve with dips.

180ml water	300g strong white bread flour,
1 teaspoon salt	plus more for rolling
1 teaspoon quick yeast	

You will need 2 large greased baking trays

Makes 12 medium pittas

1. Pour the water into the bread pan of your machine and add the salt. Put the flour on top and finally the yeast. Select the **Basic Dough** programme.

2. Once the dough is ready, turn it out onto a floured board and cut the dough into 12 equal pieces and mould each piece into a ball.

3. Using a floured rolling pin, roll each piece into an approximate oval or round shape. Roll each fairly thinly - about the thickness of a 50 pence piece - and arrange them over the baking trays. Leave to rest for about half an hour, covering each tray with a clean tea towel.

4. Heat your oven to a high setting - around 220°C (fan ovens) or equivalent.

5. Bake the pittas for about 2-4 minutes until puffed and risen. If you wish, you can turn them over halfway through baking but it's quite a hot and dangerous process and you don't want to lose too much heat from your oven through opening the door.

6. Remove from the baking tray to a serving plate or basket and cover with a clean tea towel to keep the pittas moist as they cool.

Wholemeal Pitta Bread

using main recipe

Prepare the dough as for the main recipe but swap 100g of the white flour for wholemeal flour.

Party Pittas

using main recipe

Prepare the dough as for either of the previous versions but divide into 24 pieces to make mini pittas. Bake for 2-4 minutes until puffed and risen.

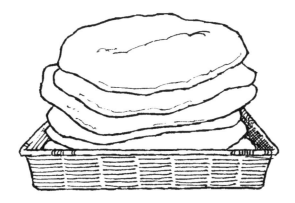

Candied Bacon

If you haven't tried this before, it's quite a revelation and very moreish. You can use it as an ingredient to make some tasty loaves and rolls or as a garnish for a dinner or supper dish: it's good scattered over soups and salads. Start with a small amount and see if you like it: you can always double or triple quantities next time if it becomes a favourite.

1. Line a large baking tray with greaseproof paper (it's advisable not to skip this stage or you will be soaking your baking tray in soapy water for the next week) and lightly grease a grill rack that will fit over the top.

2. Preheat your oven to a high setting – 220-230°C (fan oven) or equivalent.

3. You will need approximately **3–4 rashers unsmoked back bacon**. Trim away most of the fat as it tends to scorch.

4. Rinse the bacon in a little cold water and shake off all of the excess.

5. Put **about 75g soft brown sugar** into a shallow dish and rub each slice of bacon on both sides with the sugar, patting it into place. Lay the sugared bacon on the rack.

6. Put the bacon into the oven immediately and bake for 10-20 minutes until sticky and crisp, turning it over halfway through the cooking time.

7. Drain on kitchen paper and cut into 1cm squares or matchsticks.

Candied Bacon Loaf

This makes an unusual and tasty loaf and is especially good with soup and tomato-based pasta dishes.

Approximately 100g candied bacon, diced

300ml warm water

2 tablespoons mild oil

1 teaspoon salt

1 tablespoon sugar

400g strong white bread flour

1 teaspoon quick yeast

You will need a large greased baking tray

1. Make sure the bacon is dry and free from grease.

2. Pour the water and oil into the bread pan of your machine and add the salt and sugar, placing them at different ends of the pan. Put the flour on top and finally the yeast. Select the **Basic Dough** programme.

3. Once the dough is ready, flour your hands and turn it onto a floured board. Knead it into a ball and roll it out to a depth of about 2½cm. Pat it all over to eliminate any air bubbles.

4. Scatter the bacon pieces over the surface of the rolled out dough, spacing them out fairly evenly.

5. Roll up the dough as tightly as you can into a long sausage. Tuck the two ends underneath. This will reveal a nice smooth top – you will then find it surprisingly easy to manoeuvre it into a round bun shape.

6. Transfer to the prepared baking tray and leave it to prove until it has almost doubled in size.

7. Preheat your oven to your usual bread-baking temperature of 180–220°C (fan oven) or equivalent. Bake for around 30 minutes until golden brown.

8. Leave on the tray for a few moments and transfer to a wire rack to cool. A clean tea towel over the top will keep the loaf moist as it cools.

If the flour to liquid ratio doesn't seem quite right for your machine, in that the amount of liquid seems too great, try increasing the total flour measurement to 500g and decrease the water to 260ml. Check with your machine's instruction booklet recipes to see the typical flour to liquid ratio for your machine.

Corn Bread

Traditionally, authentic American corn bread is made with baking powder but this pale, creamy yellow version with yeast is delicious. It is great for breakfast or teatime or served with a bowl of chilli con carne.

You could use polenta but the texture will be quite different and discernibly 'bitty'. Polenta is cornmeal but more coarsely ground – giving more of a characteristic grittiness than the finer cornmeal.

300ml water	300g strong white bread flour
2 tablespoons mild oil	100g finely ground cornmeal
1 teaspoon salt	1 teaspoon quick yeast
1 tablespoon sugar	

You will need a greased 450g loaf tin

1. Pour the water and oil into the bread pan of your machine and add the salt and sugar, placing them at different ends of the pan. Put the flour and cornmeal on top and finally the yeast. Select the **Basic Dough** programme.

2. Once the dough is ready, remove it from the machine with lightly floured hands and knead it briefly on a floured board.

3. Mould it into an approximate oval shape and put it into the prepared loaf tin. Leave to prove until almost doubled in size.

4. Preheat your oven to your usual bread-baking temperature of 180–220°C (fan oven) or equivalent. Bake for around 30 minutes until golden brown.

5. Leave to settle and contract away from the sides of the tin for a few minutes and then transfer to a wire rack to cool.

If the flour to liquid ratio doesn't seem quite right for your machine, in that the amount of liquid seems too great, try increasing the total flour/cornmeal measurement to 500g and decrease the water to 260ml. Check with your machine's instruction booklet recipes to see the typical flour to liquid ratio for your machine.

Corn Bread Muffins

using main recipe

These are easy to prepare and look very appealing. They are handy for picnics and lunch boxes.

Makes 12

You will need a greased 12-cup muffin tin

1. Prepare the dough as for the main recipe.

2. Once the dough is ready, turn it out onto a lightly floured board, knead it briefly and cut the dough into 12 equal pieces: roll each piece between your cupped hands until you have a smooth ball.

3. Put a piece into each cup of the prepared muffin tin. Leave to prove until almost doubled in size.

4. Preheat the oven to 180–220°C (fan oven) or equivalent. Bake for 8–10 minutes until golden brown.

5. Leave in the tin for a few moments to cool and contract and then remove and finish cooling on a wire rack. A clean tea towel over the top will keep the muffins fresh and moist as they cool.

Corn Bread Muffins in Frills

using main recipe

The muffin cases look appealing and hold the dough in so that it forms a higher domed shape.

Makes 12

You will need a 12-cup muffin tin lined with muffin-size paper cases and a small saucer of mild oil

1. Prepare the dough as for the main recipe.

2. Once the dough is ready, turn it out onto a lightly floured board, knead it briefly and cut the dough into 12 equal pieces: roll each piece between your cupped hands until you have a smooth ball.

3. Dip each ball of dough to about halfway up in the oil, shake off any excess and put into the paper cases in the muffin tin. This will prevent the muffins sticking to the paper cases once baked. Leave to prove until almost doubled in size.

4. Preheat the oven to 180-220°C (fan oven) or equivalent. Bake for 8-10 minutes until golden.

Baby Corn Bread Loaves

using main recipe

These look particularly appealing and unusual. They are lovely to make for children or as something a bit different for guests.

Makes 12

You will need 12 greased mini-loaf tins (the kind you can buy in packs of four)

1. Prepare the dough as for the main recipe.

2. Once the dough is ready, turn it out onto a lightly floured board, knead it briefly and cut the dough into 12 equal pieces. Put a piece into each prepared mini-loaf tin, turning each piece to reveal a smooth top.

3. Place the tins on a baking tray to make it easier to lift them in and out of the oven. Leave to prove until almost doubled in size.

4. Preheat the oven to 180–220°C (fan oven) or equivalent. Bake for 8–10 minutes until golden brown.

5. Leave in the tins for a few moments to cool and contract; you should then be able to just lift them out of their tins. Finish cooling on a wire rack. A clean tea towel over the top will keep the loaves fresh and moist as they cool.

Home-made Pizza

Home-made pizzas are hard to beat. It's easy to make your own dough by hand but even easier in a bread machine.

Makes 2

210ml water	½ teaspoon sugar
1 tablespoon mild oil	300g strong white bread flour
1 teaspoon salt	½ teaspoon quick yeast

You will need 2 pizza pans, approximately 30cm in diameter, or 2 large baking trays, greased

1. Pour the water and oil into the bread pan of your machine and add the salt and sugar, placing them at different ends of the pan. Put the flour on top and finally the yeast, positioning it on top. Select the **Pizza Dough** programme.

2. Once the dough is ready, turn it onto a lightly floured board, knead it briefly and cut it into two.

3. Flour your hands and roll the first piece into a ball and then flatten into a disc. Use a lightly floured rolling pin to help you. If the dough seems quite elastic and pings back, allow it to relax a few moments and then continue.

4. When you have got a fairly flat disc, lift it onto your rolling pin and transfer it to the pizza pan or tray. Repeat with the second piece.

5. Cover both pieces loosely with greaseproof paper and leave to rise on the trays for about an hour in a warm place.

6. After about an hour, set the oven to a high setting – 220–230°C (fan ovens) or equivalent – and put on the topping of your choice.

Topping suggestions
Good-quality pasta sauce from a jar or your own home-made
Mozzarella cheese, drained of whey

Whatever else you fancy, such as:

Sliced mushrooms
Sliced ham
Sliced salami or pepperoni
Anchovies
Olives
Capers
Pineapple
Jalapeno peppers
Sliced red, green and yellow peppers
Sliced chilli peppers
Egg (see below)
Freshly ground black pepper
Oregano, fresh or dried

7. Start with the tomato sauce; just spread it on quite thinly, you don't want too much. Arrange the rest of your chosen toppings over the sauce. If you are going to put an egg on top leave a clear space in the middle.

8. Baking time depends very much on your oven but, as a guide, bake for 10–12 minutes. If you are having an egg on top, bake for 7–8 minutes and then remove carefully from the oven, closing the oven door immediately. Crack the egg in the middle of the pizza and return to the oven for 3–4 minutes.

Suggested topping combinations
Although you can go down the 'everything on it' route you might prefer slightly more themed toppings: ham and mushroom, ham and pineapple, and so on.

You can't go wrong with **simple cheese and tomato**. Spread the **tomato sauce** sparingly over the base and top with slices of **mozzarella**. Grind a little **black pepper** over the top and add a sprinkling of **dried oregano**. You could also use grated Cheddar instead of mozzarella for a simple family meal.

Add a fancy restaurant touch by scattering **fresh rocket leaves** or **basil leaves** over your pizza immediately before serving, or have some on the table for people to help themselves.

Another great combination is **pepperoni, jalapeno and fried egg on a wholemeal base.** Make up the pizza dough with 250g of **strong white flour** and 50g **wholemeal flour.** Spread the base with **tomato sauce** and top with **mozzarella.** Arrange slices of **pepperoni** on top of that, leaving a clear space in the middle for the **egg.** Add a few sliced **jalapeno peppers** from a jar. Bake for 7-8 minutes, remove from the oven, crack your egg into the space in the middle and return to the oven for 3-4 minutes.

Pizza Puttanesca

If you eat pizza a lot and feel like a change of topping, try this one based on a well-known pasta sauce.

1 red chilli	Roughly 75g black pitted olives
1 clove garlic	1–2 teaspoons pickled capers, drained
1 x 50g tin of anchovy fillets in oil	Mozzarella cheese, drained of whey
1 x 400g tin of plum tomatoes	

1. Fry the chilli and garlic gently in oil from the anchovies. Snip half of the anchovy fillets into small pieces and add to the pan. Stir so that the anchovies break up completely and cook gently. Break up the tomatoes with a fork, remove any skin or central core and add to the pan. Chop half of the olives into small pieces and add to the pan with the capers. Stir everything together and simmer gently for half an hour or so.

2. When you are ready to bake the pizza, spread the topping over the base (don't feel you have to use it all, if you have any left over it will keep in the fridge for a couple of days, to use over pasta later). Slice some mozzarella over the top and arrange the rest of the olives and anchovies on top of that. Bake for 10-12 minutes.

Breakfast Pizza

You could make these breakfast-themed pizzas for a late weekend breakfast/ early lunch.

Makes 2

Good-quality pasta sauce from a jar or your own home-made
A couple of slices of ham, snipped into pieces and/or a couple of butcher's quality sausages, already cooked and sliced

Approximately 100g mushrooms, sliced
4 eggs
Freshly ground black pepper

1. Make up the pizza dough as for the main recipe with 250g of strong white flour and 50g wholemeal flour. Divide into two and proceed as before.

2. Spread the bases with tomato sauce.

3. Arrange the mushrooms, ham and slices of sausage, if using, on top, leaving two clear spaces on each pizza for the eggs.

4. Bake for 7–8 minutes, remove from the oven, crack your eggs into the spaces and return to the oven for 3–4 minutes. Season with black pepper and serve.

Flat Garlic Bread with or without Oregano

These are delicious with or without oregano and make a good appetiser to serve to guests with drinks or with home-made pasta for a relaxed weekend lunch. Use a pizza cutter to mark into wedges.

Makes 2

210ml water

1 tablespoon olive oil

1 teaspoon salt

½ teaspoon sugar

300g strong white bread flour

½ teaspoon quick yeast

1 tablespoon dried oregano (or to taste), if using

Plain melted butter plus melted garlic butter for spreading

You will need 2 pizza pans, approximately 30cm (12in) in diameter or 2 large baking trays, greased

1. Pour the water and oil into the bread pan of your machine and add the salt and sugar. Put the flour on top and the yeast. Add the oregano, if using. Select the **Pizza Dough** programme.

2. Once the dough is ready, turn it onto a lightly floured board and cut it into two. Flour your hands and roll the first piece into a ball and then flatten into a disc. Use a lightly floured rolling pin to help you.

3. When you have got a flat disc, lift it onto your rolling pin and transfer it to the pizza pan or tray. Repeat with the other piece.

4. After about an hour, set the oven to a high setting – 220°C (fan ovens) – and brush or spread lightly with the plain butter.

5. Depending upon how thinly you have rolled the dough, bake for 10–15 minutes until puffed and golden. Brush or spread immediately with the garlic butter, cut the bread into wedges and serve.

Note: The garlic butter isn't put on before baking as the intense heat of the oven would scorch the tiny pieces of garlic and they would become burnt and bitter.

To make garlic butter
Use quantities to suit. Mix some **softened butter** with some **finely sliced garlic clove** or a little **minced garlic from a jar.**

To freeze pizza dough
It's handy to have some pizza bases in the freezer and it's simple to freeze home-made ones. Roll into discs as before. Interleave with greaseproof paper and place on a piece of cardboard – a flattened cereal box is ideal. Seal securely inside a plastic bag, making sure all air has been eliminated, and freeze flat. Defrost before using.

Pasta Dough

Fresh, home-made pasta tastes wonderful and it's easy and fun to make – especially if you have a pasta rolling machine. The best and most traditional way to make the dough is on a large board or table, incorporating the water or egg into the flour by hand.

However, you do need plenty of time – and, crucially, plenty of clearing up time – when you use this method, and it's sometimes the thought of all the clearing up that can put you off the whole operation.

You can still make delicious fresh pasta at home without quite so much upheaval by mixing the pasta dough in your bread machine. You may have a machine with a specific pasta programme but if you are using the **Pizza Dough** programme you will only need to run the dough cycle for 20-30 minutes.

Whole Egg Pasta

4 eggs   400g plain flour (or pasta flour)

1. Put the eggs into the bread pan and the flour on top. Select the **Dough** programme.

2. Keep an eye on things and run the programme for 20-30 minutes until the dough has formed into a smooth, compact ball and then switch off. You may need to hold the switch down for several seconds before it engages. (Some machines may need a helping hand with a flexible spatula in the early stages of mixing to ensure all the flour is incorporated into the dough.)

3. Transfer the dough to a bowl, cover and leave to rest for half an hour.

4. Follow the instructions for your pasta rolling machine.

3

Sweet Loaves, Buns and Tea Breads

With the aid of your bread machine you will soon be turning out sweet loaves, buns and tea breads worthy of the classiest patisserie.

See Chapter 2, 'Dough Recipes', for more general dough information.

PROGRAMMES

Your machines will have a selection of different types of programmes, usually including:

- a **Basic Dough** programme useful for the majority of doughs you will make;

- a **Raisin Dough** option will be useful for when you are adding dried fruit and so on where the pieces are to remain entire rather than broken up and incorporated into the mixture.

ORDER OF INGREDIENTS

When adding the ingredients to the bread pan, the most important aspect to bear in mind is to keep the yeast dry and away from the salt and sugar in the very first stages.

The preferred method for adding ingredients is usually to put the liquid in first, the salt and the sugar spaced apart, then the flour and the yeast on top last of all. This works well with most machines and is particularly helpful with the occasional machine that struggles slightly to gather up all the flour into the dough ball during the initial mixing.

If in doubt, add the ingredients in the order specified by your instruction book.

Note: If you have no raisin beep or raisin dispenser, knead the fruit into the dough once it is ready and you have taken it out of the machine. Add it a little at a time.

FLOUR TO LIQUID RATIOS

An alternative amount of flour and liquid is suggested for some recipes. The second amount may be better suited to the more competitively priced makes of bread machine, which tend to use a greater proportion of flour to liquid.

Mixtures containing significant quantities of moist fruit or vegetable such as apple, banana and so on, tend to perform successfully in most types of machine without altering the original amounts of flour and liquid in the mixture. The final amount of dough may be slightly smaller in volume when made in the more competitively priced machines.

Richer, brioche-type mixtures containing generous quantities of butter and egg also tend to perform successfully in most types of machine without altering the original amounts of flour and liquid in the mixture. Again, the final amount of dough may be slightly smaller in volume when made in the more competitively priced machines.

Always use the measuring spoon that comes with your bread machine for both dry and liquid ingredients; and always fill the spoons to the top and level off dry ingredients.

Check with your machine's instruction booklet to see the typical flour to liquid ratio for your machine.

Currant Buns

Main recipe

This is a useful recipe to have in your repertoire for a delicious 'everyday bun'.

Makes 12

260ml warm water	400g strong white bread flour
1 egg	1 teaspoon yeast
2 tablespoons mild oil	150g currants, raisins, sultanas, mixed
1 teaspoon salt	A little melted butter for finishing
25g caster sugar	

You will need a greased baking tray

1. Pour the water, egg and oil into the bread pan of your machine and add the salt and sugar, placing them at different ends of the pan. Put the flour on top and finally the yeast.

2. Select the **Dough** programme with **Raisin option** – either put the fruit in the raisin compartment, if your machine has one, or wait for, or set, the raisin beep and add it when it sounds. The finished dough will be quite soft so flour your hands before you take it out of the machine and keep the board and rolling pin lightly floured throughout.

3. Once the dough is ready, turn it out onto a floured board, knead briefly and cut the dough into 12 equal pieces.

4. Mould each piece into rounds: roll it between your cupped hands until you have a smooth ball. Place on a greased baking tray and leave to prove until almost doubled in size.

5. Towards the end of this time, preheat the oven to 180-220°C (fan ovens) or equivalent.

6. Bake for 8-10 minutes or until golden brown. Remove from the oven and brush with melted butter while still warm. Alternatively, finish with 'Sticky Glaze'. Cool on a wire rack.

If you have no raisin beep or raisin dispenser, knead the fruit into the dough once it is ready and you have taken it out of the machine. Add it a little at a time.

If the flour to liquid ratio doesn't seem quite right for your machine, in that the amount of liquid seems too great, try increasing the flour to 500g and decrease the water to 230ml. Check with your machine's instruction booklet recipes to see the typical flour to liquid ratio for your machine.

To make a sticky glaze

You can turn your buns into 'sticky buns' with this delicious, easy glaze. Heat 2 **tablespoons of caster sugar** and 2 **tablespoons of water** together in a small heavy-bottomed pan until all the sugar is melted and bubbling. Brush the glaze over the buns and allow them to cool before serving.

Buns in a Bun Tin

using Main Currant Bun Recipe

Makes 12

You will need a greased 12-cup muffin tin

1. Make the dough as for the main recipe.

2. Once the dough is ready, turn it out onto a floured board, knead briefly and cut the dough into 12 equal pieces.

3. Mould each piece into a round between your cupped hands until you have a smooth ball. Put each one into the prepared tin as soon as you have shaped it. Leave to prove until almost doubled in size. The buns will rise to fit the tin.

4. Preheat the oven to 180–220°C (fan oven) or equivalent and bake for 8–10 minutes until golden.

Currant Buns in Corsets

using Main Currant Bun Recipe

The paper cases make the buns look appealing but also have a practical use: they act as a kind of corset to make them rise in a more uniform domed shape.

Makes 12

You will need a 12-cup muffin tin lined with muffin-size paper cases and a small saucer of mild oil

1. Prepare the buns as for the previous recipe. Dip each piece of dough to about halfway up in the oil, shake off any excess and put into the paper cases in the muffin tin. This will prevent the buns sticking to the paper cases once baked. The buns will rise to fit the cases.

2. Leave to prove until almost doubled in size.

3. Preheat the oven to 180–220°C (fan oven) or equivalent and bake for 8–10 minutes until golden.

Currant Bun Round

Make a most appealing and professional-looking round of buns by arranging them in a large round loose-bottomed cake tin.

1. Make the dough as for the main recipe, knead briefly, divide into 12 and mould into balls as before. Put 9 pieces round the outside of a 23cm round cake tin in a ring and 3 in the middle. As they rise they will join together.

2. Leave to prove until almost doubled in size and joined together. Preheat the oven to 180-220°C (fan oven) or equivalent and bake for around 25-30 minutes or until golden brown.

3. Leave to settle for a while and then remove in one piece and cool on a wire rack. A clean tea towel over the top will keep the buns fresh and moist as they cool.

4. Brush with the **sticky glaze** (see main recipe) for a final professional flourish.

Hot Cross Buns

Hot cross buns seem to arrive in the shops shortly after Christmas these days, but originally they were made especially to eat on Good Friday. People would sometimes save a hot cross bun for the whole of the following year, either to hang up in the house to keep them safe from harm, or to eat a small piece of it if illness struck. You can make these spiced fruit buns with the traditional crosses on for Easter and make them plain for the rest of the year.

Makes 12

For the buns

260ml warm water	400g strong white bread flour
1 egg	1 teaspoon yeast
2 tablespoons of mild oil	1 teaspoon mixed spice
1 teaspoon salt	150g currants, raisins, sultanas, mixed
25g unrefined caster sugar	25g candied peel, diced

For the bakers' mixture for crosses

50g plain flour	5ml oil
Pinch of baking powder	1 egg, beaten with a teaspoon of water
50ml cold water	

You will need a greased baking tray

1. Pour the water, egg and oil into the bread pan of your machine and add the salt and sugar, placing them at different ends of the pan. Put the flour on top and finally the yeast and mixed spice – keep the yeast and spice at opposite sides of the bread pan.

2. Select the **Dough** programme with **Raisin option** – either put the fruit and candied peel in the raisin compartment, if your machine has one, or wait for, or set, the raisin beep and add them when it sounds.

3. Once the dough is ready, turn it out onto a lightly floured board, knead briefly and cut the dough into 12 equal pieces. Lightly mould each piece into a ball by rolling it between your cupped hands. Place on a greased baking tray and leave to prove until almost doubled in size.

4. Towards the end of this time, preheat the oven to 180-220°C (fan ovens) or equivalent.

5. Meanwhile, make the mixture for the crosses by mixing the flour, baking powder and water to a smooth paste, and stir in the oil. Spoon the mixture into a piping bag with a plain nozzle.

6. Brush each bun with beaten egg and pipe a thin cross onto each one.

7. Bake for 8-10 minutes or until the buns are golden brown. Remove from the oven and cool on a wire rack.

If you have no raisin beep or raisin dispenser, knead the fruit into the dough once it is ready and you have taken it out of the machine. Add it a little at a time.

If the flour to liquid ratio doesn't seem quite right for your machine, in that the amount of liquid seems too great, try increasing the flour to 500g and decrease the water to 230ml. Check with your machine's instruction booklet recipes to see the typical flour to liquid ratio for your machine.

Malted Milk Buns

These delicious squidgy buns are a bit like little round golden malt loaves. Split them and eat with butter. If you have any left after a couple of days they are gorgeous toasted: cut them in half and toast them lightly on both sides under the grill – they are too fat to go in the toaster!

You can buy jars of barley malt extract in most health food shops. Incidentally, a teaspoonful or two of malt extract stirred into warm milk at bedtime makes a soothing and relaxing drink.

Makes 12

300ml warm milk	1 teaspoon salt
2 tablespoons mild oil	500g strong white bread flour
1 egg	1½ teaspoons yeast
4 tablespoons barley malt extract (or 2 tablespoons barley malt extract and 2 tablespoons runny honey)	150g raisins and sultanas, mixed

About 2 tablespoons runny honey to glaze

You will need a greased 12-cup muffin tin

1. Pour the milk into the bread pan of your machine with the oil and add the egg, malt extract and salt. Put the flour on top and finally add the yeast.

2. Set the machine to the **Dough** programme with **Raisin option** – either put the fruit in the raisin compartment, if your machine has one, or wait for, or set, the raisin beep and add it when it sounds.

3. Once the dough is ready, flour your hands and transfer it to a floured board: the dough will be quite soft and sticky.

4. Knead the dough lightly and divide into 12 equal pieces. Mould each piece into a ball by rolling it between your floured cupped hands and put them in the prepared muffin tin. Leave to prove until almost doubled in size.

5. Preheat the oven to 180-220°C (fan oven) or equivalent and bake for around 10 minutes until golden brown.

6. While the buns are baking, warm the honey, either in a saucepan or for about 20 seconds in the microwave on High.

7. Once the buns are baked, leave them to settle for a few moments and remove to a wire rack. Brush with the warmed honey and leave to cool.

Measuring Malt Extract: Measure the oil first and use the still oily spoon to measure the malt extract – this ensures it will slide off the spoon easily. An oiled spoon works well for measuring honey, syrup and treacle as well.

If you have no raisin beep or raisin dispenser, knead the fruit into the dough once it is ready and you have taken it out of the machine. Add it a little at a time.

If the flour to liquid ratio doesn't seem quite right for your machine, in that the amount of liquid seems too great, try increasing the flour to 550g and decrease the milk to 260ml. Check with your machine's instruction booklet recipes to see the typical flour to liquid ratio for your machine.

Plum Bread

This is a lovely old-fashioned fruit loaf. It doesn't actually contain any plums or even prunes; the word 'plum' refers to the drying process known as plumming. Many years ago 'plums' meant any kind of dried fruit.

Serve this sliced thinly and spread with butter for a delicate afternoon tea, or slice it more thickly for a substantial snack. It is also good toasted the following day and great with thin slices of cheese.

140ml warm water	300g strong bread flour
2 tablespoons mild oil	½ teaspoon quick yeast
1 egg	100g raisins, currants and sultanas, mixed
1 teaspoon salt	25g candied peel, finely chopped (optional)
1 tablespoon caster sugar	
A little melted butter for glazing	

You will need a greased 450g loaf tin

1. Pour the water into the bread pan of your machine with the oil and add the egg, followed by the salt and sugar, placing them at different ends of the pan. Put the flour on top and finally add the yeast.

2. Select the **Dough** programme with **Raisin option** – either put the fruit and candied peel in the raisin compartment, if your machine has one, or wait for, or set, the raisin beep and add them when it sounds.

3. Once the dough is ready, flour your hands and turn it onto a floured board. Knead it lightly and roll it around the board with one hand to get a smooth shape. Lift it into the prepared tin. Don't worry about shaping further it as it will expand to fit the tin as it rises. Leave it to rise until it has almost doubled in size.

4. Once it has risen sufficiently preheat the oven to 180–220°C (fan ovens) or equivalent. Bake for approximately 30 minutes until golden brown.

5. Remove the loaf from the oven and leave it in the tin for a few minutes to cool and contract slightly before you turn it out. Brush with melted butter while still warm.

6. Cool on a wire rack. Cover with a clean tea towel to keep it moist as it cools.

If you have no raisin beep or raisin dispenser, knead the fruit into the dough once it is ready and you have taken it out of the machine. Add it a little at a time.

This recipe is suitable for most types of bread machine.

Fruit Tea Bread

This is delicious plain or toasted at breakfast or teatime. It's also good to take on picnics or as part of a packed lunch.

300ml warm freshly brewed tea:
Earl Grey works well
2 tablespoons mild oil
1 egg
1 teaspoon salt

1 tablespoon caster sugar
400g strong white bread flour
1 teaspoon yeast
150g mixed raisins, sultanas and currants

You will need a greased 450g loaf tin

1. Pour the tea into the bread pan of your machine with the oil and add the egg, followed by the salt and sugar, placing them at different ends of the pan. Put the flour on top and finally add the yeast.

2. Set the machine to the **Dough** programme with **Raisin option** - either put the fruit in the raisin compartment, if your machine has one, or wait for, or set, the raisin beep and add it when it sounds.

3. Once the dough is ready, flour your hands and turn it onto a floured board. Knead it lightly and roll it around the board with one hand to get a smooth shape. Lift it into the prepared tin. Don't worry about shaping further it as it will expand to fit the tin as it rises. Leave it to rise until it has almost doubled in size.

4. Once it has risen sufficiently preheat the oven to 180-220°C (fan ovens) or equivalent and bake for approximately 30 minutes until browned and ready.

5. Remove the loaf from the oven and leave it in the tin for a few minutes to cool and contract slightly before you turn it out. Cool on a wire rack. Cover with a clean tea towel to keep it moist as it cools.

If you have no raisin beep or raisin dispenser, knead the fruit into the dough once it is ready and you have taken it out of the machine. Add it a little at a time. If the flour to liquid ratio doesn't seem quite right for your machine, in that the amount of liquid seems too great, try increasing the flour to 500g and decrease the tea to 260ml. Check with your machine's instruction booklet recipes to see the typical flour to liquid ratio for your machine.

Fruited Apple Buns

These rise beautifully, have a lovely fresh flavour and keep well.

Makes 12

160ml warm water	25g unrefined caster sugar
2 tablespoons mild oil	400g strong white bread flour
175g grated apple	1 teaspoon yeast
1 teaspoon salt	150g currants, raisins, sultanas, mixed

You will need a greased baking tray

1. Pour the water, oil and grated apple into the bread pan of your machine and add the salt and sugar, placing them at different ends of the pan. Put the flour on top and finally the yeast. Set the machine to the **Dough** programme with **Raisin option** - either put the fruit in the raisin compartment, if your machine has one, or wait for, or set, the raisin beep and add it when it sounds.

2. Once the dough is ready, turn it out onto a lightly floured board and knead it briefly. Cut the dough into 12 equal pieces and lightly mould each piece into a ball by rolling it between your cupped hands. Place on a greased baking tray and leave to prove until almost doubled in size.

3. Towards the end of this time, preheat the oven to 180-220°C (fan ovens) or equivalent.

4. Bake for 8-10 minutes or until golden brown. Remove from the oven and cool on a wire rack.

If you have no raisin beep or raisin dispenser, knead the fruit into the dough once it is ready and you have taken it out of the machine. Add it a little at a time.

This recipe is suitable for most types of bread machine.

Bara Brith (Welsh Tea Bread)

This is a version of the popular fruit bread served as part of a traditional Welsh tea. Bara brith means 'speckled bread' – that is to say, bread speckled with dried fruit. Originally, it was made by adding dried fruit to the usual bread dough and over time it was enriched further with fat, sugar and occasionally an egg. The reference to 'tea' sometimes means simply that the fruit bread is eaten at teatime but it is also sometimes actually made with tea, so replace the water with the same amount of tea if you prefer. Use freshly brewed tea that has been allowed to cool to lukewarm. Bara brith has many interpretations: some families even make theirs with diluted orange squash as the liquid!

Eat it sliced fairly thickly and spread with butter for tea. Eat it fresh the first day and, after that, lightly toasted; it's lovely for breakfast.

The honey glaze is a nice touch, but it's not essential. If you are not fond of candied peel, or don't have any to hand, leave it out and make the total weight of currants and raisins up to 125g instead.

300ml warm water or tea (see above)	400g strong bread flour
50g block vegetable shortening or lard, diced	1 teaspoon yeast
	100g currants and raisins, mixed
1 egg	25g candied peel, finely chopped
1 teaspoon salt	
2 tablespoons sugar	Plus approximately 2 tablespoons clear honey to glaze

You will need a greased 450g loaf tin

1. Pour the water or tea into the bread pan of your machine with the lard or vegetable shortening and egg. Add the salt and sugar, placing them at different ends of the pan. Put the flour on top and finally add the yeast. Set the machine to the **Dough** programme with **Raisin option** – either put the fruit in the raisin compartment, if your machine has one, or wait for, or set, the raisin beep and add it when it sounds.

2. Once the dough is ready, flour your hands and turn it onto a floured board. Knead it lightly and roll it around the board with one hand to get a smooth shape. Lift it into the prepared tin. Leave it to rise until it has almost doubled in size.

3. Once the dough has nearly risen sufficiently, turn on your oven to 180-220°C (fan oven) or equivalent and once it has come to temperature, bake for approximately 30 minutes until browned and ready.

4. Remove the loaf from the oven and leave for a few minutes to cool and contract slightly before you turn it out. Brush with the honey while it is still warm, and cool on a wire rack. Once completely cold, store in an airtight container and eat within a couple of days. Alternatively, brush the loaf with melted butter while still warm.

If you have no raisin beep or raisin dispenser, knead the fruit into the dough once it is ready and you have taken it out of the machine. Add it a little at a time.

If the flour to liquid ratio doesn't seem quite right for your machine, in that the amount of liquid seems too great, try increasing the flour to 500g and decrease the water to 280ml. Check with your machine's instruction booklet recipes to see the typical flour to liquid ratio for your machine.

Cinnamon butter
Try any of the previous three fruit loaves lightly toasted and spread with cinnamon butter: see the recipe for **Bath Buns** on page 139 for details of how to make it.

Tea Cakes

These are gorgeous eaten fresh with butter, although obviously the main idea is to have them split and toasted.

Makes 10

300ml warm water	450g strong bread flour
35g lard or block vegetable shortening, diced	1 teaspoon quick yeast
	150g of mixed currants, raisins and sultanas
1 teaspoon salt	
1 tablespoon sugar	A little milk for glazing

You will need 1 or 2 greased baking trays

1. Put the water and lard or vegetable shortening into the bread pan of your machine. Add the salt and sugar, placing them at different ends of the pan. Put the flour on top and finally the yeast. Select the **Dough** programme with **Raisin option** – either put the fruit in the raisin compartment, if your machine has one, or wait for, or set, the raisin beep and add it when it sounds.

2. Once the programme has finished put the dough onto a floured board, knead it briefly and divide into 10 pieces.

3. Mould into balls by rolling each piece of dough between your cupped hands and flatten gently with your hands. Space them out onto the greased baking tray(s), and leave to rise until they have almost doubled in size. Depending on the room temperature, this could be round about an hour.

4. Brush the tops gently with milk and bake in a preheated oven at 180-220°C (fan oven) or equivalent for approximately 10 minutes or until golden brown. Cool on a wire rack.

If you have no raisin beep or raisin dispenser, knead the fruit into the dough once it is ready and you have taken it out of the machine. Add it a little at a time. This recipe is suitable for most types of bread machine.

Alternative glaze
Instead of brushing the tea cakes with milk before they go into the oven to give them a light glaze, you may prefer to brush them with melted butter after they come out of the oven. This will give them a light glaze and also keep the tops soft.

Griddled Tea Cakes

Here's a novel way to toast your tea cakes.

1. Preheat the grill so that the grill rack is very hot.

2. Split the tea cakes and roll each half with a rolling pin so that they are quite thin and flat and bigger in circumference.

3. Carefully press the tea cakes onto the grill rack and toast lightly. Turn over and repeat on the other side.

4. Serve immediately with butter.

Lavender and Honey Buns

This recipe is based on the **Lavender and Honey Bread** recipe in Chapter 2 and is replicated here for convenience.

If you can find prettily patterned paper muffin cases the buns will look even more appealing.

Makes 12

15–20 sprigs of lavender flowers still in bud	1 teaspoon salt
300ml warm water	1 tablespoon runny honey
2 tablespoons mild oil	400g strong white bread flour
	1 teaspoon quick yeast

You will need a 12-cup muffin tin and 12 muffin-size paper cases and a saucer of mild oil

1. Lay the lavender sprigs on kitchen paper for a while to dry out. Remove all the florets from the stalks and shake them lightly in a sieve.

2. Pour the water and oil into the bread pan of your machine and add the salt and honey, placing them at different ends of the pan. Put the flour on top and finally the yeast. Set the machine to the **Dough** programme with **Raisin option** – either put the lavender in the raisin compartment, if your machine has one, or wait for, or set, the raisin beep and add the lavender when it sounds.

3. Once the dough is ready, turn it out onto a lightly floured board and knead it briefly. Cut the dough into 12 equal pieces and lightly mould each piece into a ball by rolling it between your cupped hands.

4. Dip each ball of dough to about halfway up in the oil, shake off any excess and put into the paper cases in the muffin tin. This will prevent the muffins sticking to the paper cases once baked. Leave to prove until almost doubled in size.

5. Preheat the oven to 180-220°C (fan oven) or equivalent and bake for 8-10 minutes until golden.

If you have no raisin beep or raisin dispenser, knead the lavender into the dough once it is ready and you have taken it out of the machine. Add it a little at a time.

If the flour to liquid ratio doesn't seem quite right for your machine, in that the amount of liquid seems too great, try increasing the flour to 500g and decrease the water to 260ml. Check with your machine's instruction booklet recipes to see the typical flour to liquid ratio for your machine.

Panettone-style Buns

These little buns are based on the Italian panettone. It's important to say that they are in the *style* of panettone rather than *actual* panettone: it is quite a long-drawn-out process to make the genuine article in Italy and involves a lot of skill and experience. Nevertheless, these are lovely and especially good dressed up at Christmas time with a dusting of icing sugar and a few ribbons. The muffin tin gives them just the right traditional shape.

Makes 12

140ml warm water	1 teaspoon salt
2 tablespoons mild oil	2 tablespoons caster sugar
1 egg	300g strong bread flour
1 egg yolk	½ teaspoon quick yeast
1 teaspoon of vanilla extract or	100g raisins and sultanas, mixed
vanilla bean paste	50g candied peel, finely chopped
Finely grated zest of 1 lemon	

You will need a greased 12-cup muffin tin

1. Put the water, oil, egg, egg yolk, vanilla and lemon zest into the bread pan of your machine and add the salt and sugar, placing them at different ends of the pan. Put the flour on top and finally the yeast.

2. Set the machine to the **Dough** programme with **raisin option** – either put the fruit and candied peel in the raisin compartment, if your machine has one, or wait for, or set, the raisin beep and add them when it sounds. The finished dough will be quite soft and sticky so flour your hands before you take it out of the machine and keep the board and rolling pin lightly floured throughout.

3. Once the dough is ready, turn it out onto a floured board and divide into 12 equal pieces. Lightly mould each piece into a ball by rolling it between your cupped hands and drop into the muffin tin: they will expand to fit perfectly as they rise. Leave the buns in a warm place until they have almost doubled in size.

4. Preheat the oven to 150°C (fan oven) or equivalent and bake for 7 minutes and then turn down the heat to 130°C or equivalent and bake for a further 3 minutes.

5. Remove from the oven and leave in the tin for a few moments then transfer to a wire rack to finish cooling. Dust with icing sugar; ideally, use vanilla icing sugar (see below).

If you have no raisin beep or raisin dispenser, knead the fruit into the dough once it is ready and you have taken it out of the machine. Add it a little at a time.

Vanilla icing sugar
Store newly purchased vanilla pods in a jar of icing sugar. You can easily dust off the pods when you need to use them and they will have left a lovely lingering vanilla scent in the icing sugar. Although you can rinse and pat dry used vanilla pods to store in granulated and caster sugar, any trace of moisture will cause icing sugar to clump and cake, so it's better to use perfectly dry ones.

Plain Panettone-style Buns and Orange Buns

You can make a plainer version of the previous recipe if you aren't fond of dried fruit. Simply proceed as before but leave out the dried fruit and candied peel.

Alternatively, make a light and beautifully flavoured orange version by leaving out the dried fruit, candied peel, lemon zest and vanilla extract and adding instead the **finely grated zest of one orange**.

Instead of dusting with icing sugar after baking, as for the previous recipe, brush the tops of the buns gently with **leftover beaten egg white** just before they go into the oven. This will give them a nice sheen. Be careful not to carry the egg white down the sides, though, or you will effectively 'glue' the buns into the muffin tin!

The orange buns are perfect for relaxed holiday breakfasts and are particularly nice served at Christmas time as a contrast to heavier fare. If you have guests, and the time to bake two batches, a mixed plate of Orange Buns and Chocolate Breakfast or Elevenses Buns make a welcome combination.

Panettone-style Cake

using main recipe

If you like, you can try your hand at one large panettone.

1. Make the dough as for the previous recipe, knead it lightly, mould it into one large round and put it into a greased 18cm loose-bottomed cake tin.

2. Let it rise in a warm place until it has doubled in size and looks almost the right size for the finished cake. Bake for 10 minutes at 150°C and then turn the heat down to 130°C and bake for a further 15 minutes.

3. Leave to settle for a few moments, then remove from the tin. Cool on a wire rack and dust with icing sugar; try using vanilla icing sugar (see previous recipe for details).

4. If it's Christmas time or another special occasion, decorate with a suitable ribbon. Candles also look festive, particularly the taller, more slender and tapered type of birthday candle.

Chelsea Buns

Chelsea buns huddle together as a joined batch, which gives them their characteristic 'rounded square' shape. They are perfect for elevenses with a cup of coffee: dunking should definitely be allowed.

Makes 12

For the dough

160ml warm water	25g butter, diced
1 egg	1 teaspoon salt
1 egg yolk (keep the white for finishing the buns; beat it lightly first)	1 tablespoon caster sugar
	350g strong bread flour
	½ teaspoon quick yeast

For the filling

100g sultanas, raisins and currants, mixed	25g caster sugar
25g butter, diced	½ teaspoon mixed spice

You will need a greased baking tray

1. Pour the water into the bread pan of your machine with the egg, egg yolk and butter. Add the salt and sugar, placing them at different ends of the pan. Put the flour on top and finally the yeast. Select the **Dough** programme.

2. When the dough is almost ready, put all the filling ingredients into a small saucepan and heat gently until the butter has melted, the sugar has dissolved and the fruit is plumping up a little. Leave to cool.

3. Once the dough is ready, knead it lightly on a floured board. Divide it into two equal pieces: it's a good idea to weigh both pieces and adjust them if they are unequal.

4. Roll each piece into a long rectangle measuring around 30–35cm in length and spread the cooled fruit mixture down the centre of each rectangle, using the back of a dessertspoon to help you. Brush the end of the dough furthest away from you (the short side of the rectangle) with the egg white.

5. Roll up each piece like a Swiss roll: start rolling with the end that has not been brushed with egg white (the other short side of the rectangle). As you roll, spread the fruit out almost to the edges of the dough for good fruit coverage. When you finish rolling, press gently onto the strip of egg white to seal, and rest the roll with the sealed edge tucked underneath.

6. Cut each roll into 6 slices. Transfer the slices to the prepared baking tray, placing them cut side down and close together but not actually touching – they will join together as they rise.

7. You may find the end pieces a little light on fruit and that some fruit strays out of the middle pieces. If this is the case, carefully tuck any stray fruit into the end pieces. Leave to prove and join together until puffed and risen and touching each other. If you have any beaten egg white left you can brush it gently over the buns just before baking to give them a nice sheen.

8. Preheat the oven to 180-220°C (fan oven) or equivalent and bake for approximately 8-10 minutes or until golden brown. Remove from the tray with a broad palette knife or fish slice and cool on a wire rack. Cover with a clean tea towel to keep the buns moist as they cool.

These are great as they are, slightly warm, or you may like to drizzle them with a little **lemon glacé icing** once they are cold. Alternatively, drizzle with **sticky glaze** from the currant bun recipes. Chelsea buns are at their best eaten very fresh.

Lemon Glacé Icing
The lemon juice takes the edge off the sweetness. Sieve **225g icing sugar** into a large bowl and stir in **2 tablespoons lemon juice** (sieve it through a tea strainer first). Beat with a wooden spoon until glossy.

Breakfast Buns

These taste a little bit like small Danish pastries or those *petits pains aux raisins* that are so lovely for a relaxing holiday breakfast with a cup of tea or coffee. The method for making these is very much simpler, though: it's done by making the dough extra rich with proportionally more butter and eggs. The dough is a richer version of the Chelsea bun dough.

Makes 12

For the dough

130ml warm water	25g butter, diced
1 egg	1 teaspoon salt
1 egg yolk (keep the white for finishing the buns; beat it lightly first)	1 tablespoon caster sugar
	300g strong bread flour
	½ teaspoon quick yeast
½ teaspoon vanilla extract or vanilla bean paste	

For the filling

100g sultanas, raisins and currants, mixed	25g butter
	25g caster sugar

You will need a large greased baking tray

1. Pour the water into the bread pan of your machine and add the egg, egg yolk, vanilla and butter. Add the salt and sugar, placing them at different ends of the pan. Put the flour on top and finally the yeast. Select the **Dough** programme.

2. When the dough is almost ready, put all the filling ingredients into a small saucepan and heat gently until the butter has melted, the sugar has dissolved and the fruit is plumping up a little.

3. The finished dough will be quite soft and sticky, so flour your hands before you take it out of the machine and keep the board and rolling pin lightly floured throughout.

4. Once the dough is ready, knead it lightly on a floured board. Divide it into two equal pieces: it's a good idea to weigh both pieces and adjust them if they are unequal.

5. Roll the pieces into long rectangles measuring around 30-35cm in length.

6. Cool the fruit and butter mixture and spread down the centre of each of the two pieces of dough, using the back of a dessertspoon to help you. Brush the end of the dough furthest away from you (the short side of the rectangle) with the egg white.

7. Roll up each piece like a Swiss roll: start rolling with the end that has not been brushed with egg white (the other short side of the rectangle). When you finish rolling, press gently onto the strip of egg white to seal.

8. Cut each roll into 6 slices. Transfer the slices to the prepared baking tray, placing them cut side down and close together but not actually touching – they will join together as they rise.

9. A fish slice can be useful to help manoeuvre the rolls from the work surface to the baking tray. Leave to prove until puffed and risen. If you have any beaten egg white left you can brush it gently over the buns just before baking to give them a nice sheen.

10. Preheat the oven to 180-220°C (fan oven) or equivalent and bake for approximately 8-10 minutes, until golden. Remove from the tray with a broad palette knife or fish slice and cool on a wire rack.

Feel free to dunk one of these in a cup of milky or frothy coffee – go on, no one's looking!

Chocolate Breakfast or Elevenses Buns

These are not unlike *petits pains au chocolat*, but much easier to make. Proceed in exactly the same way as for the previous recipe, but instead of the fruit filling, scatter approximately **80g of chopped dark chocolate (or half milk, half dark)** down the centre of each length of dough. Continue as before.

Alternatively, instead of laying the slices cut side down like a piece of Swiss roll, sit them upright, sealed edge down.

This recipe should work in most types of machine, producing a soft, slightly sticky dough.

If you have a very efficient bread machine that uses a lower proportion of flour to liquid, you may like to try cutting the amount of flour from 300g to 250g for an even richer dough.

Bath Buns

You may not be able to take tea and buns in the glorious setting of the Pump Room in Bath, to the strains of classical music very often, but with the aid of your bread machine you can make a very good version of a Bath bun at home. There's nothing to stop you tuning your radio to some soothing music and dreaming while you eat your bun.

Makes 12

140ml warm water	1 teaspoon salt
1 egg	2 tablespoons caster sugar
1 egg yolk (keep the white for finishing the buns; beat it lightly first)	300g strong bread flour
	½ teaspoon quick yeast
	75g raisins and sultanas, mixed
50g butter, diced	25g candied peel, finely chopped

4 or 5 white sugar lumps, crushed in a pestle and mortar

You will need a large greased baking tray

1. Put the warm water, egg, egg yolk and butter into the bread pan. Add the salt and sugar, placing them at different ends of the pan. Put the flour on top and finally the yeast. Set the machine to the **Dough** programme with **Raisin option** – either put the fruit and candied peel in the raisin compartment, if your machine has one, or wait for, or set, the raisin beep and add them when it sounds.

2. Once the dough is ready, lightly flour your hands and turn it out onto a floured board. Divide the dough equally into 12 pieces, mould gently into rounds between your cupped palms, and put them onto the prepared baking tray; the dough will be quite rich and soft to the touch. Leave them in a warm place until they are practically half as big again.

3. Brush gently with the beaten egg white and sprinkle with the crushed sugar lumps. Bake in a preheated oven at your normal bread baking temperature of 180-220°C (fan oven) or equivalent for approximately 8-10 minutes or until golden brown.

These are fabulous eaten fresh and warm, just as they are, or with a touch of butter or cinnamon butter. They are still lovely the next day but that nice little contrast has gone between the ever so slightly crisp firmness of the outside of the bun and the squidgy softness inside. In any event, eat within a couple of days.

A note on the sugar topping: If you have had a genuine Bath bun you will have noticed the special sugar on top. It must be a closely guarded baker's secret as it doesn't seem to be available in the shops. Sugar lumps crushed in a pestle and mortar is a good alternative; if you can get hold of the more irregular-shaped cane sugar lumps, these work better. White sugar on top of the buns seems more traditional, but brown sugar lumps are appealing too.

If you have no raisin beep or raisin dispenser, knead the fruit into the dough once it is ready and you have taken it out of the machine. Add it a little at a time.

This recipe should work in most types of machine, producing a soft, slightly sticky dough.

Cinnamon Butter

This is perfect to accompany your Bath buns. Stir a little **icing sugar** and a similar amount of **cinnamon** into **softened butter**. Don't add too much: just enough to flavour the butter slightly without being overpowering.

Big Bath Bun

This is exactly the same dough as for the recipe above, but instead of forming it into the traditional small buns, mould it into one big bun. It does look quite comical, as it looks exactly the same as the regular ones but 12 times as big. It's a bit like looking at one of those outsize versions of yellow plastic bathtime ducks; you are so used to the smaller ones, they are strangely unexpected.

1. Make the dough as above. Once it is ready, ease the dough out of the bread pan with floured hands onto a lightly floured board. Mould into a flattish round and ease onto a greased baking tray.

2. You may need to smooth it out a bit more. At this stage it should measure roughly 20cm across (if you make it too deep and domed the middle won't cook through properly). Leave it in a warm place to rise until it is practically half as big again and, although still fairly flat, fractionally more domed in appearance.

3. Once it has risen sufficiently, brush the top gently with beaten egg white and water as in the previous recipe and sprinkle with crushed sugar lumps: two or three lumps will be plenty.

4. Bake in a preheated oven at your normal bread baking temperature of 180-220°C (fan oven) or equivalent for around 25 minutes until golden brown.

5. Slice the bun thickly and eat on its own or spread with butter or cinnamon butter. If you have any left the next day you can eat it with butter and apricot preserve, or toast it lightly under the grill.

Helpful note: When you are baking sweet buns and loaves on a baking tray you may find it helpful to line the tray. Greaseproof paper works well: grease the tray first, cut a piece of the paper to fit and smooth it over the tray.

If sticky deposits of fruit and sugar have oozed out onto your baking trays, try soaking the tray in warm water with a dishwasher tablet. Any stubborn bits can be rubbed gently afterwards with another dishwasher tablet and a tiny amount of water.

Iced Buns

These are simply iced **Bridge Rolls** from Chapter 2, 'Dough Recipes'. Iced buns are popular with most people but especially with small children; in fact, this is a fun recipe to make with children.

It's nice to colour half the icing pink and have half the buns with pink icing and half with white. There's no need to resort to food colouring: just use a dab of raspberry jam. Iced bun icing needs to have that extra sticky, slightly stretchy quality; the glycerine provides that effect. The lemon juice prevents the icing from tasting overpoweringly sweet.

Bake a batch of Bridge Rolls from the recipe in Chapter 2 and leave to cool on a wire rack.

Glacé icing (with extra sticky properties)

175g icing sugar
2–3 tablespoons lemon juice
3 teaspoons glycerine

A small spoonful of seedless raspberry jam
– enough to tint the icing the exact
shade you want – or try bramble jelly for
a more lilac tone

1. Sieve the icing sugar into a roomy bowl and stir in 2 tablespoons of lemon juice and the glycerine. Work the icing sugar into the liquid with a wooden spoon and add the rest of the lemon juice as necessary; it shouldn't be too runny.

2. Once the rolls are completely cold, spoon half of the icing onto six of the rolls. Use a teaspoon and spread and smooth the icing along the length of the roll with the back of the spoon. Stir the jam into the rest of the icing and ice the other six rolls.

3. Eat very fresh.

Helpful note: Sometimes you might want to make up a half quantity of icing and ice half the batch, leaving the rest as plain rolls.

Iced Bun Round

Make a round of iced buns by arranging them in a 23cm round loose-bottomed cake tin. These are similar to the previous recipe but round and baked in a round batch. If you decorate each bun with glacé cherry (either a whole or a half) they will look even more professional – as if fresh from a high street baker's shop.

300ml water	1 tablespoon sugar
2 tablespoons mild oil	400g strong white bread flour
1 teaspoon salt	1 teaspoon yeast

You will need a greased 23cm round loose-bottomed cake tin

1. Pour the water and oil into the bread pan of your machine and add the salt and sugar, placing them at different ends of the pan. Put the flour on top and finally the yeast. Select the **Basic Dough** programme.

2. Once the dough is ready, turn it out onto a floured board and cut into 12 equal pieces. Lightly mould each piece into a ball by rolling it between your cupped hands.

3. Put 9 pieces round the outside of the cake tin in a ring and 3 in the middle. As they rise they will join together.

4. Leave to prove until almost doubled in size and joined together. Bake in a preheated oven at 180-220°C (fan oven) or equivalent, for around 25-30 minutes or until golden brown.

5. Leave to settle for a while and then remove in one piece and cool on a wire rack. A clean tea towel over the top will keep the buns fresh and moist as they cool.

6. Once cold, ice with the glacé icing from the Iced Bun recipe.

If the flour to liquid ratio doesn't seem quite right for your machine, in that the amount of liquid seems too great, try increasing the flour to 500g and decrease the water to 260ml. Check with your machine's instruction booklet recipes to see the typical flour to liquid ratio for your machine.

Chocolate Bread

Main recipe

This unusual semi-sweet bread is light in texture with a deep and satisfying chocolate flavour. It seems a natural partner to milky coffee and is good to offer guests for breakfast or elevenses. Eat as it is or lightly buttered. The chocolate flavour also works well with marmalade, black cherry or raspberry jam, or sliced banana.

You can either bake the bread as one large round loaf in a cake tin or as an appealing bun round. Try the bun round as a centrepiece for a weekend breakfast table and serve with cups of milky coffee – dunking should definitely be encouraged.

Slices of the loaf version make fabulous open-faced sandwiches with black cherry jam and mascarpone. Use the mascarpone plain or stir in a little vanilla extract and icing sugar to taste. Once the bread is a day old try it lightly toasted or as the basis for a chocolate bread and butter pudding.

240 ml warm milk	1 teaspoon salt
25g butter, diced	75g unrefined caster sugar
1 egg	400g strong white bread flour
1egg yolk	50g cocoa powder
2 teaspoons vanilla extract	1 teaspoon yeast

1. Pour the milk and butter into the bread pan of your machine with the egg, egg yolk and vanilla extract. Add the salt and sugar, placing them at different ends of the pan. Put the flour on top with the cocoa and finally the yeast.

2. Select the **Dough** programme.

Round Chocolate Loaf

You will need a greased 18cm round loose-bottomed cake tin

1. Once the dough is ready, remove it from the machine with lightly floured hands – it will be quite soft – and put it straight into the prepared cake tin, turning the dough so that a smooth rounded top is revealed. Leave to prove until almost doubled in size.

2. Preheat your oven to your usual bread-baking temperature of 180-220°C (fan oven) or equivalent. Just before you put the loaf in the oven, brush the top with **10g melted butter**. Bake for around 30 minutes.

3. Leave to settle and contract away from the sides of the tin for a few minutes and then transfer to a wire rack to cool.

Chocolate Bun Round

You will need a greased 23cm round loose-bottomed cake tin

1. Divide the dough into 12 equal pieces and mould each piece into a round ball between your cupped hands. Arrange the shaped pieces in the cake tin: put 9 pieces round the outside in a ring and 3 in the middle. As they rise they will join together.

2. Leave to prove until almost doubled in size. Brush with **10g melted butter** and bake in a preheated oven at 180-220°C (fan oven) or equivalent, for around 25-30 minutes or until risen and baked through, as before.

3. Leave to settle for a while and then remove in one piece and cool on a wire rack. A clean tea towel over the top will keep the buns fresh and moist as they cool.

4. Brush with melted butter while still warm.

If the flour to liquid ratio doesn't seem quite right for your machine, in that the amount of liquid seems too great, try increasing the flour to 500g and decrease the milk by 40ml. Check with your machine's instruction booklet recipes to see the typical flour to liquid ratio for your machine.

Chocolate Cinnamon Bread

The cinnamon gives the chocolate an intriguing, almost citrussy, tang.

Prepare the dough as for the main chocolate bread recipe, but leave out the vanilla extract and add **2 teaspoons of cinnamon** instead: put it on top of the flour, keeping it at the opposite end of the bread pan from the yeast.

Chocolate Fruit Bread

Prepare the dough as for the main recipe and include the vanilla extract. Add *either* **150g raisins or sultanas** *or* **150g dried cherries** (sometimes called dried sour cherries) and set the machine to the **Dough programme with Raisin option** – either put the fruit in the raisin compartment, if your machine has one, or set, or wait for, the raisin beep and add the fruit when it sounds.

If you have no raisin beep or raisin dispenser, knead the fruit into the dough once it is ready and you have taken it out of the machine. Add it a little at a time.

Chocolate Cream or Custard Cream Buns

Makes 12

You will need a 12-cup muffin tin and 12 muffin-size paper cases and a saucer of mild oil

1. Prepare the dough as for the main recipe.

2. Once the dough is ready, divide it into 12 equal pieces and mould each piece into a round ball between your cupped hands. Dip each piece of dough to about halfway up in the oil, shake off any excess and put into the paper cases in the muffin tin. This will prevent the muffins sticking to the paper cases once baked.

3. Leave to prove until almost doubled in size.

4. Preheat the oven to 180–220°C (fan oven) or equivalent and bake for around 10 minutes until risen and baked through. Transfer to a wire rack to cool.

5. Once cold, cut a slit at an angle through the top of each bun and fill with whipped cream or Custard Buttercream. Alternatively, you may like to use the Lemon and Vanilla Buttercream from the Sultana Splits recipe on page 150.

Note: If you are using whipped cream, try adding a dab of black cherry jam as well, before the cream.

Custard Buttercream

If you are fond of custard, you will love this. Be warned: it has a very moreish flavour.

50g softened butter
75g icing sugar

25g custard powder
A tablespoon of milk

1. Cream the butter in a bowl large enough to give you room to manoeuvre. Use a wooden spoon. Gradually add the icing sugar and custard powder, passing it through a sieve.

2. When the icing sugar and custard powder is all combined, stir in the milk, just enough to loosen the mixture slightly.

Banana Sultana Bread

Use bananas that are ripe but not *completely* overripe: the skin may be starting to speckle but the flesh should still be creamy white and not soft and brown. This is delicious fresh and moist, spread with butter, and after a couple of days makes great toast. It has a lovely, faintly chewy texture and is especially good for breakfast.

175g banana, peeled weight (don't add more than this, just to 'use it up' or the bread will be heavy)
160ml warm water
2 tablespoons mild oil
1 teaspoon salt
1 tablespoon sugar
400g strong white bread flour
1 teaspoon quick yeast
150g sultanas

You will need a greased 450g loaf tin

1. Mash the banana until smooth but not liquidy.

2. Pour the water and oil into the bread pan of your machine and add the salt and sugar, placing them at different ends of the pan. Put the flour on top. Add the mashed banana, and finally the yeast, positioning it on top of the flour and clear of the banana.

3. Set the machine to the **Dough** programme with **Raisin option** – either put the sultanas in the raisin compartment, if your machine has one, or wait for, or set, the raisin beep and add the sultanas when it sounds.

4. Once the dough is ready, flour your hands and turn it onto a floured board. Knead it lightly and roll it around the board with one hand to get a smooth shape. Lift it into the prepared tin. Don't worry about shaping further as it will expand to fit the tin as it rises. Leave to prove until almost doubled in size.

5. Preheat your oven to your usual bread-baking temperature of 180–220°C (fan oven) or equivalent. Bake for around 30 minutes until golden brown.

6. Leave to settle and contract away from the sides of the tin for a few minutes and then transfer to a wire rack to cool.

If you have no raisin beep or raisin dispenser, knead the fruit into the dough once it is ready and you have taken it out of the machine. Add it a little at a time.

This recipe is suitable for most types of bread machine.

Sultana Splits with Lemon and Vanilla Buttercream

These are perfect with a cup of tea mid afternoon if you've only had a very light lunch.

Makes 8

300ml water	400g strong white bread flour
2 tablespoons mild oil	1 teaspoon yeast
1 teaspoon salt	100g sultanas
1 tablespoon sugar	

You will need a large greased baking tray

1. Pour the water and oil into the bread pan of your machine and add the salt and sugar, placing them at different ends of the pan. Put the flour on top and finally the yeast.

2. Set the machine to the **Dough** programme with **Raisin option** – either put the sultanas in the raisin compartment, if your machine has one, or wait for, or set, the raisin beep and add the sultanas when it sounds.

3. Once the dough is ready, turn it out onto a floured board and knead it lightly. Divide the dough into two even pieces.

4. Mould both the pieces into rounds: do this with one hand, rolling the dough lightly against the work surface. Position them on the prepared baking tray with sufficient space between them so that they don't join together as they rise, and leave to prove until almost doubled in size.

5. Once the dough has risen, mark both pieces into quarters with a sharp knife that has a non-serrated blade: unlike the method for soda bread and farls, this time you are aiming to cut all the way through if you can.

6. Preheat the oven to 180-220°C (fan oven) or equivalent and bake for 9-10 minutes or until golden brown.

7. Remove and cool on a wire rack. A clean tea towel over the top will keep the scones fresh and moist as they cool.

8. Separate the individual scones and cut a slit in each one through the rounded edge. Fill with the buttercream: you can spoon it in with a teaspoon, or pipe it in using an icing bag or syringe fitted with a star nozzle.

9. Dust the tops lightly with icing sugar, stirring it through a tea strainer to get a nice even distribution.

10. Eat very fresh.

If you have no raisin beep or raisin dispenser, knead the fruit into the dough once it is ready and you have taken it out of the machine. Add it a little at a time.

If the flour to liquid ratio doesn't seem quite right for your machine, in that the amount of liquid seems too great, try increasing the flour to 500g and decrease the water to 260ml. Check with your machine's instruction booklet recipes to see the typical flour to liquid ratio for your machine.

Lemon and Vanilla Buttercream Icing

The lemon juice takes the edge off the sweetness and the vanilla gives a lovely depth of flavour.

50g softened butter
100g icing sugar
A squeeze of lemon juice

A few drops of vanilla extract or
¼ teaspoon of vanilla bean paste

1. Cream the butter in a bowl large enough to give you room to manoeuvre. Use a wooden spoon. Gradually add the icing sugar, passing it through a sieve.

2. When the icing sugar is all combined, add the vanilla and stir in a squeeze of lemon juice, just enough to loosen the mixture slightly.

Rhubarb Pizza

Here's something a bit different for pudding or to offer with a cup of tea or coffee – and it's very easy to prepare. Although simple, it's extremely good: not too sweet, nicely tart and satisfying. It's fine cold, but best of all served warm, fresh from the oven. Cut it into wedges: it's delicious just on its own but a dollop of cream or thick Greek yoghurt wouldn't go amiss.

The quantities for the dough will make two medium-size pizzas. If you don't want to make two rhubarb pizzas you could make one with rhubarb and one with apple, or turn the other pizza base into garlic bread to serve as an appetiser – see Chapter 2, 'Dough Recipes'.

Alternatively, you could freeze one of the bases: see below for details.

Makes 2

210ml water	½ teaspoon quick yeast
1 tablespoon mild oil	
1 teaspoon salt	Around 500g rhubarb
½ teaspoon sugar	2–3 tablespoons sugar (or to taste)
300g strong white bread flour	A splash of orange juice (or water)

A little melted butter plus more sugar for sprinkling

You will need 2 pizza pans, approximately 30cm in diameter, or 2 large baking trays, greased

1. Pour the water and oil into the bread pan of your machine and add the salt and sugar, placing them at different ends of the pan. Put the flour on top and finally the yeast, positioning it on top. Select the **Dough** programme.

2. Once the dough is ready, turn it onto a lightly floured board and cut it in two.

3. Flour your hands and roll the first piece into a ball and then flatten into a disc. You can use a lightly floured rolling pin to help you. If the dough seems quite elastic and pings back, allow it to relax for a few moments and then continue.

4. When you have got a flat disc, lift it onto your rolling pin and transfer it to the pizza pan or tray. Repeat with the second piece.

5. Cover them loosely with greaseproof paper and leave to rise on the trays for about an hour in a warm place.

6. Prepare the rhubarb and slice into chunks – diagonal chunks look attractive. Cook over a gentle heat with the sugar and orange juice or water until just tender.

7. Remove half of the rhubarb chunks from the pan and set aside. Continue to cook the rest of the rhubarb for another few minutes until completely tender. Leave to cool slightly.

8. Spread the pizza bases with melted butter. Spread the completely tender rhubarb over the bases and arrange the lightly cooked rhubarb pieces over the top. Sprinkle with sugar.

9. Preheat the oven to 220°C (fan ovens) or equivalent and bake for 10–12 minutes until the edges of the base are golden and puffy and the rhubarb is very slightly charred at the corners and caramelised.

10. Cut into wedges with a pizza cutter or a sharp knife to serve.

To freeze pizza dough
Roll into discs as before. Interleave with greaseproof paper and place on a piece of cardboard – a flattened cereal box is ideal. Seal inside a plastic bag, making sure all the air has been eliminated, and freeze flat. Defrost before using.

Apple Pizza

As with the rhubarb pizza, this is extremely simple but delicious. Best served in wedges, warm from the oven, just as it is, it's also good with a little cream or vanilla ice cream. The quantities for the dough will make two medium-size pizzas: if you don't want to make two apple pizzas you could make one with apple and one with rhubarb.

Makes 2

Approximately 500g dessert apples, such as Cox's	50g sultanas
A splash of apple juice or water	½ teaspoon cinnamon (or to taste), optional
Melted butter	Sugar for sprinkling

1. Prepare the dough as for the Rhubarb Pizza.

2. Peel and core the apples, slice finely and cook gently with the apple juice or water until the apples are tender but some texture remains. Once the juices start to run, add the sultanas. Stir in the cinnamon, if using.

3. Spread the pizza bases with melted butter. Spread the apple and sultana mixture over the bases. Sprinkle with sugar.

4. Preheat the oven to 220°C (fan ovens) or equivalent and bake for 10-12 minutes until the edges of the base are golden and puffy and the apple is slightly bubbling.

5. Cut into wedges with a pizza cutter or a sharp knife to serve.

Christmas Pizza

This is very simple to put together but deliciously Christmassy. Serve warm, but not boiling hot, as the mincemeat retains its heat for quite a while. This looks festive served just as it is or with a little cream or brandy butter on the side.

The quantities for the dough will make two medium-size pizzas: if you don't want to make two mincemeat pizzas you could make one with mincemeat and one with apple.

Makes 2

Approximately 400–500g   Melted butter
    mincemeat

1. Prepare the dough as for the Rhubarb Pizza.

2. Spread the pizza bases with melted butter and spread the mincemeat over the top.

3. Preheat the oven to 220°C (fan ovens) or equivalent and bake for 10–12 minutes until the edges of the base are golden and puffy and the mincemeat is bubbling.

4. Cut into wedges with a pizza cutter or a sharp knife to serve.

4

Easy Cakes From Your Bread Machine

MELT AND BAKE CAKES

Bread machines with the **Bake only option** are handy for making an easy cake; somehow, it seems much less effort than using the oven and it's more economical on electricity. These recipes are also useful if your oven has broken down, or if it is full of Sunday lunch, and you need to make a cake for tea. Bread machines aren't cut out for light-as-a-whisper sponge cakes, but they can help you bake a very good loaf or bar-type cake based around dried fruit, ginger and so on.

Some machines have a cake programme which will do a certain amount of the mixing for you, as well as bake the cake, but consult your machine's instruction book for recipes for these as machines vary.

Here is a small selection of recipes suitable for machines with the **Bake only option** with a **timer** for adding extra time as necessary.

All the cakes are made with largely store cupboard ingredients and take a minimum amount of preparation. With the exception of the bread pudding, which is mixed in a bowl, they involve just a bit of melting and stirring in a single large saucepan. You then pour the mixture into the bread pan of your machine. They also create a minimal amount of washing up and clearing away, which is always good news.

Before baking a cake remove the mixing blade and grease the bread pan. It is also advisable to line the bottom of the bread pan (see individual recipes for details). Always make sure the bread pan is out of the machine when you pour in the mixture. A flexible spatula will help you to scrape out every last drop. Be sure to mix the flour in gradually and thoroughly: if you are a bit slapdash you may end up with the odd little white blob of flour here and there in the finished cake.

And, finally, leave the cake to settle and begin cooling and contracting away from the sides of the bread pan before you turn it out. Again, see individual recipes for details.

In each case, select the **Bake only** programme and enter the correct time for the recipe on the **timer**. If you need to add extra time at the end, you may have to switch the machine off and on again and reselect the programme.

Please note: all cake recipes in this section use ordinary plain flour.

Dark Ginger Cake

Here's a seriously dark and sticky Jamaican Ginger type cake that adapts perfectly to the bread machine.

6 tablespoons black treacle	110g butter, diced
75g unrefined caster sugar	225g plain flour
2 teaspoons mixed spice	2 teaspoons baking powder
3 teaspoons ground ginger	2 medium eggs, lightly beaten
150ml cold water	

1. Remove the mixing blade and grease the bread pan.

2. Line the bottom of the bread pan with greaseproof paper: invert the pan on top of your paper and draw round it, avoiding the handle. Cut round the lines and snip a few cuts round the edges of the paper to enable it to lie flat against the sides of the pan. Settle the paper into the bottom of the pan and press over the blade spindle, smoothing the edges flat.

3. Put the black treacle, sugar, spices and water into a roomy pan. Heat over a moderate heat until the mixture is bubbling slightly and the sugar has dissolved. Add the butter. Continue to heat until the butter has melted.

4. Add the baking powder to the weighed flour.

5. Leave the black treacle and sugar mixture until almost cold and, using a sieve, gradually stir in half the flour and baking powder a little at a time with a wooden spoon. Add the eggs, one at a time with a little more flour, and mix in. Add the remaining flour gradually, stirring it in as you go.

6. Pour the mixture carefully into the prepared bread pan, being sure to keep pouring into the middle so that the mixture spreads out of its own accord and stays on top of the greaseproof paper. Select the **Bake only** programme and enter 1 hour on the timer.

7. Test with a skewer. It may need another 5 or 10 minutes. If so, close the lid smartly and enter another 5 or 10 minutes on the timer. Make a note for the next time.

8. When the cake is ready, switch off the machine and remove the bread pan but leave the cake in the bread pan to settle for 10 minutes or so. After that time it should have started to contract away from the sides of its own accord.

9. Protect one hand with a cloth and put your other hand carefully inside the bread pan and support the cake with your outspread fingers as you turn the bread pan upside down. The cake should come out easily. Peel away the greaseproof paper and finish cooling on a wire rack.

10. Once completely cold, store in an airtight tin.

Sticky Gingerbread Cake

This is a lovely moist and sticky gingerbread that is popular with both adults and children.

50g dark brown sugar	150ml cold water
4 tablespoons golden syrup	110g butter, diced
2 tablespoons black treacle	225g plain flour
2 teaspoons mixed spice	2 teaspoons baking powder
3 teaspoons ground ginger	2 medium eggs, lightly beaten

1. Remove the mixing blade and grease the bread pan.

2. Line the bottom of the bread pan with greaseproof paper: invert the pan on top of your paper and draw round it, avoiding the handle. Cut round the lines and snip a few cuts round the edges of the paper to enable it to lie flat against the sides of the pan. Settle the paper into the bottom of the pan and press over the blade spindle, smoothing the edges flat.

3. Put the sugar, golden syrup, black treacle, spices and water into a roomy pan. Heat over a moderate heat until everything has melted and the sugar has dissolved. Add the butter. Continue to heat until the butter has melted.

4. Add the baking powder to the weighed flour.

5. Leave the sugar mixture until almost cold and, using a sieve, gradually stir in half the flour and baking powder a little at a time with a wooden spoon. Add the eggs, one at a time with a little more flour, and mix in. Add the remaining flour gradually, stirring it in as you go.

6. Pour the mixture carefully into the prepared bread pan, being sure to keep pouring into the middle so that the mixture spreads out of its own accord and stays on top of the greaseproof paper. Select the **Bake only** programme and enter 1 hour on the timer.

7. Test with a skewer. If the cake isn't done, close the lid smartly and enter another 5 or 10 minutes on the timer. Make a note for the next time.

8. When the cake is ready, switch off the machine and remove the bread pan but leave the cake in the bread pan to settle for 10 minutes or so. After that time it should have started to contract away from the sides of its own accord.

9. Protect one hand with a cloth and put your other hand carefully inside the bread pan and support the cake with your outspread fingers as you turn the bread pan upside down. The cake should come out easily. Peel away the greaseproof paper and finish cooling on a wire rack.

10. Once completely cold, store in an airtight tin.

Date and Walnut Cake

This is a traditional old favourite that turns out well in the bread machine. It's beautiful just as it is - or, for a touch of luxury, try topping it with **Salted Caramel Buttercream** and a scattering of chopped walnuts.

225g stoned dates
225g plain flour
2 teaspoons baking powder
4 tablespoons runny honey
110g butter, diced

200ml cold water
2 medium eggs, lightly beaten
50g chopped walnuts – aim for
    each walnut half to be more
    or less quartered

1. Remove the mixing blade and grease the bread pan.

2. Line the bottom of the bread pan with greaseproof paper: invert the pan on top of your paper and draw round it, avoiding the handle. Cut round the lines and snip a few cuts round the edges of the paper to enable it to lie flat against the sides of the pan. Settle the paper into the bottom of the pan and press over the blade spindle, smoothing the edges flat.

3. Cut each date into 2 or 3 pieces and add the baking powder to the weighed flour.

4. Put the dates, honey, butter, and water into a roomy pan. Heat over a moderate heat for 3–5 minutes until the mixture is bubbling gently and the dates are plumping up nicely.

5. Leave until almost cold and, using a sieve, gradually stir in half of the flour and baking powder a little at a time with a wooden spoon. Add the eggs, one at a time with a little more flour, and mix in. Add the remaining flour gradually, stirring it in as you go, and then stir in the walnuts.

6. Pour the mixture carefully into the prepared bread pan, being sure to keep pouring into the middle so that the mixture spreads out of its own accord and stays on top of the greaseproof paper. Select the **Bake only** programme and enter 1 hour on the timer.

7. Test with a skewer. If the cake isn't done, close the lid smartly and enter another 5 or 10 minutes on the timer. Make a note for the next time.

8. When the cake is ready, switch off the machine and remove the bread pan but leave the cake in the bread pan to settle for 10 minutes or so. After that time it should have started to contract away from the sides of its own accord.

9. Protect one hand with a cloth and put your other hand carefully inside the bread pan and support the cake with your outspread fingers as you turn the bread pan upside down. The cake should come out easily. Peel away the greaseproof paper and finish cooling on a wire rack.

10. Once completely cold, store in an airtight tin.

Salted Caramel Buttercream Topping

If you have a jar of dulce de leche to hand, try this luxurious topping.

50g softened butter   2 level tablespoons dulce de leche
100g icing sugar   Scant ¼ teaspoon Maldon salt

About a tablespoon of chopped walnuts

1. Cream the butter in a bowl large enough to give you room to manoeuvre. Use a wooden spoon. Gradually add the icing sugar, passing it through a sieve. When all the icing sugar is combined, stir in the dulce de leche and salt.

2. Spread over the top of the cooled cake and scatter with chopped walnuts.

Date and Honey Cake

Here is a nut-free version of the previous cake that's usually more popular with children. The date and honey flavours work beautifully together.

225g stoned dates
4 tablespoons runny honey
110g butter, diced
200ml cold water

225g plain flour
2 teaspoons baking powder
2 medium eggs, lightly beaten

1. Remove the mixing blade and grease the bread pan.

2. Line the bottom of the bread pan with greaseproof paper: invert the pan on top of your paper and draw round it, avoiding the handle. Cut round the lines and snip a few cuts round the edges of the paper to enable it to lie flat against the sides of the pan. Settle the paper into the bottom of the pan and press over the blade spindle, smoothing the edges flat.

3. Cut each date into 2 or 3 pieces. Put the dates, honey, butter and water into a roomy pan. Heat over a moderate heat for 3–5 minutes until the mixture is bubbling gently and the dates are plumping up nicely.

4. Add the baking powder to the weighed flour.

5. Leave the fruit mixture until almost cold and, using a sieve, gradually stir in half of the flour and baking powder a little at a time with a wooden spoon. Add the eggs, one at a time with a little more flour, and mix in. Add the remaining flour gradually, stirring it in as you go.

6. Pour the mixture carefully into the prepared bread pan, being sure to keep pouring into the middle so that the mixture spreads out of its own accord and stays on top of the greaseproof paper. Select the **Bake only** programme and enter 1 hour on the timer.

7. Test with a skewer. If the cake isn't done, close the lid smartly and enter another 5 or 10 minutes on the timer. Make a note for the next time.

8. When the cake is ready, switch off the machine and remove the bread pan but leave the cake in the bread pan to settle for 10 minutes or so. After that time it should have started to contract away from the sides of its own accord.

9. Protect one hand with a cloth and put your other hand carefully inside the bread pan and support the cake with your outspread fingers as you turn the bread pan upside down. The cake should come out easily. Peel away the greaseproof paper and finish cooling on a wire rack.

10. Once completely cold, store in an airtight tin.

Dark Fruit and Spice Cake

Here's a traditional dark fruit bar cake that adapts well to the bread machine.

300g dried fruit: raisins, sultanas and currants
110g soft dark brown sugar
75g butter, diced
1 teaspoon mixed spice

100ml cold water
150g plain flour
2 teaspoons baking powder
2 medium eggs, lightly beaten

1. Remove the mixing blade and grease the bread pan.

2. Line the bottom of the bread pan with greaseproof paper: invert the pan on top of your paper and draw round it, avoiding the handle. Cut round the lines and snip a few cuts round the edges of the paper to enable it to lie flat against the sides of the pan. Settle the paper into the bottom of the pan and press over the blade spindle, smoothing the edges flat.

3. Put the dried fruit, sugar, butter, mixed spice and water into a roomy pan. Heat over a moderate heat for 3–5 minutes until the mixture is bubbling gently, the sugar has dissolved and the fruit is plumping up nicely.

4. Add the baking powder to the weighed flour.

5. Once the fruit mixture is almost cold, using a sieve, gradually stir in half of the flour and baking powder a little at a time with a wooden spoon. Add the eggs, one at a time with a little more flour, and mix in. Add the remaining flour gradually, stirring it in as you go.

6. Spoon the mixture carefully into the prepared bread pan, being sure to keep pouring into the middle so that the mixture spreads out of its own accord and stays on top of the greaseproof paper. Also, be sure to keep stirring the mixture left in the pan as you go, to make sure the fruit is evenly distributed throughout. Select the **Bake only** programme and enter 50 minutes on the timer.

7. Test with a skewer. If the cake isn't done, close the lid smartly and enter another 5 or 10 minutes on the timer. Make a note for the next time.

8. When the cake is ready, switch off the machine and remove the bread pan but leave the cake in the bread pan to settle for 10 minutes or so. After that time it should have started to contract away from the sides of its own accord.

9. Protect one hand with a cloth and put your other hand carefully inside the bread pan and support the cake with your outspread fingers as you turn the bread pan upside down. The cake should come out easily. Peel away the greaseproof paper and finish cooling on a wire rack.

10. Once completely cold, store in an airtight tin.

Easy Christmas Cake

At Christmas time you could top the **Dark Fruit and Spice Cake** with marzipan and icing for a speedy, no-fuss Christmas cake that's ideal for a small gathering or to give as a gift. You can make your own marzipan in the bread machine too, if you like – whatever next! See the following recipe for details.

Bread Machine Marzipan

Amazingly, you can use the dough programme of your bread machine to make beautifully fresh and almondy marzipan with the minimum of fuss. Make sure your bread pan is sparklingly clean with no trace of dough or crumbs.

Christmas cake has never been so easy!

110g icing sugar
225g ground almonds
1 very fresh egg yolk, medium
   to large in size

½ teaspoon almond extract
3 tablespoons lemon juice

1. Sieve the icing sugar into a bowl and stir in the ground almonds to combine.

2. Put the egg yolk, almond extract and lemon juice into the bread pan of your machine and add the combined icing sugar and ground almonds.

3. Select the **Dough** programme. You are aiming to run the programme for around 15 minutes, not much more than that, and it could be less in some machines.

4. Stay close to the machine and keep an eye on things: you will probably need to scrape the mixture down from the sides of the pan a couple of times with a flexible spatula.

5. As soon as the mixture comes together in the pan, stop the programme *immediately* otherwise the marzipan will become oily and overprocessed.

6. Take the mixture from the bread pan, gathering up any loose crumbs, and shape it into a ball. Wrap it in cling film and store in a cool, dry place or the fridge until needed. Allow the marzipan to come to room temperature before rolling.

Note: In some machines you may need to keep the on/off switched pressed for a few seconds before it engages.

Simple Glacé Icing

Use shop-bought ready-to-roll icing if you prefer but this is very easy and tastes delicious.

110g icing sugar

Approximately 2 tablespoons lemon juice, sieved through a tea strainer

You will need a large palette knife

1. Sieve the icing sugar into a large bowl. Make a well in the middle and pour in the lemon juice.

2. Using a wooden spoon gradually stir the juice into the icing sugar until it is all mixed in. When it is all incorporated keep stirring until it is smooth and glossy. It should be fairly stiff but still just pourable.

ICING THE CAKE

For a speedy glaze for the marzipan to sit on, spread the top only of the cake with a little marmalade, peel removed.

1. Lightly dust your work surface and rolling pin with icing sugar and shape and roll the marzipan into a broad rectangle the same size as the top of your cake. Lift onto the glazed cake and smooth gently with your rolling pin, pat down the edges and neaten with a sharp knife.

2. Once the marzipan is in place, spoon or pour some of the icing on top, positioning it down the centre and spreading it outwards to the edges with a small palette knife. Add more icing as needed. Leave the iced cake in a cool, dry place for the icing to harden slightly.

Light Fruit Cake

This is a version of the old-fashioned granny or granny's cake. Instead of the usual round shape, it has been adapted into a loaf cake to work in the bread machine but it still has the traditional sugar sprinkled on top.

225g dried fruit: currants, raisins and plenty of sultanas
110g light soft brown sugar (or unrefined granulated sugar)
110g butter, diced
200ml cold water
225g plain flour
2 teaspoons baking powder
2 medium eggs, lightly beaten
A teaspoonful or so of either sugar for sprinkling

1. Remove the mixing blade and grease the bread pan.

2. Line the bottom of the bread pan with greaseproof paper: invert the pan on top of your paper and draw round it, avoiding the handle. Cut round the lines and snip a few cuts round the edges of the paper to enable it to lie flat against the sides of the pan. Settle the paper into the bottom of the pan and press over the blade spindle, smoothing the edges flat.

3. Put the dried fruit, sugar, butter and water into a roomy pan. Heat over a moderate heat for 3–5 minutes until the mixture is bubbling gently, the sugar has dissolved and the fruit is plumping up nicely.

4. Add the baking powder to the weighed flour.

5. Leave the fruit mixture until almost cold and, using a sieve, gradually stir in half the flour and baking powder a little at a time with a wooden spoon. Add the eggs, one at a time with a little more flour, and mix in. Add the remaining flour gradually, stirring it in as you go.

6. Pour the mixture carefully into the prepared bread pan, being sure to keep pouring into the middle so that the mixture spreads out of its own accord and stays on top of the greaseproof paper. Select the **Bake only** programme and enter 1 hour on the timer.

7. Test with a skewer. If the cake isn't done, close the lid smartly and enter another 5 or 10 minutes on the timer. Make a note for the next time.

8. When the cake is ready, switch off the machine and remove the bread pan but leave the cake in the bread pan to settle for 10 minutes or so. After that time it should have started to contract away from the sides of its own accord.

9. Protect one hand with a cloth and put your other hand carefully inside the bread pan and support the cake with your outspread fingers as you turn the bread pan upside down. The cake should come out easily. Peel away the greaseproof paper and finish cooling on a wire rack. Sprinkle with sugar while still warm.

10. Once completely cold, store in an airtight tin.

Sugared almond topping

For an alternative topping try combining a couple of sugar lumps, crushed in a pestle and mortar, with approximately one tablespoon of flaked almonds. If you can get hold of the more irregular-shaped cane sugar lumps, these work better and the brown ones are even more appealing. Sprinkle over the cake before baking, concentrating particularly on the centre section.

Sugar and spice topping

You could also top the cake with a couple of crushed sugar lumps combined with ¼ teaspoon of cinnamon or mixed spice. Sprinkle over the cake before baking, concentrating particularly on the centre section. Try mixing things up a little with your own special spice combination.

Sticky Chocolate Cake

A slice of this is very welcome with a cup of tea or coffee and is popular with children. It also works well as a pudding with a scoop of vanilla ice cream.

6 tablespoons golden syrup	25g cocoa powder
50g soft dark brown sugar	2 teaspoons baking powder
150ml cold water	2 medium eggs, lightly beaten
110g butter, diced	1 teaspoon vanilla extract
200g plain flour	

1. Remove the mixing blade and grease the bread pan.

2. Line the bottom of the bread pan with greaseproof paper: invert the pan on top of your paper and draw round it, avoiding the handle. Cut round the lines and snip a few cuts round the edges of the paper to enable it to lie flat against the sides of the pan. Settle the paper into the bottom of the pan and press over the blade spindle, smoothing the edges flat.

3. Put the golden syrup, sugar and water into a roomy pan. Heat fairly gently until the mixture is bubbling slightly and the sugar has dissolved. Add the butter. Continue to heat until the butter has melted. Put aside to cool.

4. Weigh the flour and then add the cocoa and the baking powder to the correct weight of flour.

5. Leave the sugar mixture until almost cold and, using a sieve, gradually stir in half the combined flour, cocoa and baking powder a little at a time with a wooden spoon. Add the eggs, one at a time with a little more of the flour and cocoa, and mix in. Stir in the vanilla. Add the remaining flour and cocoa gradually to the mixture, stirring it in as you go.

6. Pour the mixture carefully into the pan, being sure to keep pouring into the middle so that the mixture spreads out of its own accord and stays on top of the greaseproof paper. Select the **Bake only** programme and enter 1 hour on the timer.

7. Test with a skewer. If the cake isn't done, close the lid smartly and enter another 5 or 10 minutes on the timer. Make a note for the next time.

8. When the cake is ready, switch off the machine and remove the bread pan but leave the cake in the bread pan to settle for 10 minutes or so. After that time it should have started to contract away from the sides of its own accord.

9. Protect one hand with a cloth and put your other hand carefully inside the bread pan and support the cake with your outspread fingers as you turn the bread pan upside down. The cake should come out easily. Peel away the greaseproof paper and finish cooling on a wire rack.

10. Once completely cold, store in an airtight tin.

Fruit Tea Bread

This makes an appetising-looking, fragrant fruit loaf that tastes delicious. It is quite unusual in that, apart from minute possible traces in the flour, the only fat comes from the yolk in the eggs.

You can experiment with different dried fruit and spice combinations: make up your own mixture from stoned prunes, stoned dates, apricots, apples, pears and currants, raisins, sultanas and cranberries, and add either mixed spice or cinnamon or half of each.

This slices well and is perfect with a reviving cup of tea. If you aren't actively trying to avoid fat, try it lightly buttered; it's also good with cheese.

400g mixed dried fruit selected from the following: stoned prunes, stoned dates, apricots, apple, pear, cranberries, currants, raisins and sultanas

110g soft dark brown sugar

2 teaspoons mixed spice or cinnamon

160ml tea, freshly brewed

225g plain flour

2 teaspoons baking powder

2 medium eggs, lightly beaten

1. Remove the mixing blade and grease the bread pan.

2. Line the bottom of the bread pan with greaseproof paper: invert the pan on top of your paper and draw round it, avoiding the handle. Cut round the lines and snip a few cuts round the edges of the paper to enable it to lie flat against the sides of the pan. Settle the paper into the bottom of the pan and press over the blade spindle, smoothing the edges flat.

3. Cut any prunes, dates or apricots into 2 or 3 pieces and any dried apple or pear into similar sized pieces. Put the dried fruit, sugar and spice into a roomy pan and pour in the tea. Bring to a gentle simmer over a moderate heat and allow to bubble for 3–5 minutes until the sugar has dissolved and the fruit is plumping up.

4. Add the baking powder to the weighed flour.

5. Leave the fruit mixture until almost cold and, using a sieve, gradually stir in half the flour and baking powder a little at a time with a wooden

spoon. Add the eggs, one at a time with a little more flour, and mix in. Add the remaining flour gradually, stirring it in as you go: it will be quite a stiff mixture.

6. Spoon the mixture carefully into the prepared bread pan, keeping it inside the greaseproof paper, and smooth the top down lightly with the back of a metal spoon – wetting the spoon is helpful. Select the **Bake only** programme and enter 50 minutes on the timer.

7. Test with a skewer. If the cake isn't done, close the lid smartly and enter another 5 or 10 minutes on the timer. Make a note for the next time.

8. When the cake is ready, switch off the machine and remove the bread pan but leave the cake in the bread pan to settle for 10 minutes or so. After that time it should have started to contract away from the sides of its own accord.

9. Protect one hand with a cloth and put your other hand carefully inside the bread pan and support the cake with your outspread fingers as you turn the bread pan upside down. The cake should come out easily. Peel away the greaseproof paper and finish cooling on a wire rack.

10. Once completely cold, store in an airtight tin.

Bread Pudding

Although possibly not a potential winner in the most beautiful cake competition, this is a handy recipe to have in your repertoire and a fairly economical one. You can use brown or white bread or a fruited loaf or a mixture, but all are best without the crusts and preferably a day or two old. If you find yourself making this regularly, play with the spice a little: add more, or less, or make up a spice mix according to your own personal preference.

Serve warm with custard as a pudding or cold as a cake. A wedge of bread pudding is handy for picnics and lunch boxes as it travels well and makes very few crumbs.

250g bread, crusts cut off	175–200g dried fruit: currants, raisins and
250ml cold milk	sultanas
1 medium egg, lightly beaten	2 teaspoons mixed spice (or to taste)
50g unrefined caster sugar	

1. Remove the mixing blade and grease the bread pan.

2. Line the bottom of the bread pan with greaseproof paper: invert the pan on top of your paper and draw round it, avoiding the handle. Cut round the lines and snip a few cuts round the edges of the paper to enable it to lie flat against the sides of the pan. Settle the paper into the bottom of the pan and press over the blade spindle, smoothing the edges flat.

3. Crumble the bread into small pieces. Put into a bowl with enough room to manoeuvre and pour in the milk. Stir thoroughly and leave to soak for around half an hour.

4. Mix in the egg with a dinner fork, making sure the mixture is fairly smooth with no large pieces of bread.

5. Weigh the dried fruit and sugar, measure the spice and mix them all together briefly with your hand before adding them to the mixture. Stir everything together thoroughly.

6. Spoon the mixture carefully into the prepared bread pan, keeping it inside the greaseproof paper, and smooth the top down lightly with the back of a

metal spoon. Select the **Bake only** programme and enter 1 hour on the timer.

7. Test with a skewer. If the pudding isn't done, close the lid smartly and enter another 5 or 10 minutes on the timer. Make a note for the next time.

8. When the bread pudding is ready, switch off the machine and remove the bread pan but leave the pudding in the bread pan to settle for 10 minutes or so. After that time it should have started to contract away from the sides of its own accord.

9. Protect one hand with a cloth and put your other hand carefully inside the bread pan and support the pudding with your outspread fingers as you turn the bread pan upside down. The pudding should come out easily. Peel away the greaseproof paper and finish cooling on a wire rack.

10. Once completely cold, store in an airtight tin.

CAKES FOR THE FREEZER

Any of the cakes in this section will freeze well. It's handy to be able to freeze cakes for a future occasion and it's simple to do. However, it's vitally important to wrap them well to keep the air out and protect them from freezer burn.

Make sure the cake is completely cold and wrap it closely in greaseproof paper or baking parchment. Wrap again in aluminium foil and seal inside a freezer bag. Don't forget to label; although you probably feel certain now that you will remember what it is, by the time you come to defrost the cake you may have forgotten completely!

Most freezer manufacturers suggest freezing cakes for up to three months but check with your own freezer manufacturer's recommendations.

To defrost
Remove all the wrappings and defrost the cake at room temperature.

5

Bread Debriefing

It's heartbreaking when eagerly anticipated bread turns out poorly. Don't panic, it's all a learning experience and you are bound to have a few false starts: the learning curve is always steeper at the beginning of any new venture.

Sometimes things can go awry simply because the weather is too hot and sultry (overexcited, sloppy dough, apt to collapse) or too cold (unresponsive, insufficiently risen dough) or the flour is from a new season's wheat harvest that has been grown in less than ideal conditions.

Below are some of the main things that can go amiss.

The bread is like a small shrunken rock

In the case of a loaf baked entirely in the machine, you may have actually forgotten to put the yeast in – it's all too easily done. It's a good idea to line up your ingredients beforehand so you can tell whether or not you have added them all.

In the case of wholemeal bread, you may have used a programme other than the **Whole wheat** programme: always use the **Whole wheat** programme for bread baked entirely from wholemeal flour. In the case of bread you have made with the dough cycle and baked in the oven, it may be that you didn't allow the bread time to prove sufficiently before baking: this step is essential.

Other most likely reasons may be:

♦ The yeast is no longer active – it may be old and past its use by date, or it could have come into contact with liquid or salt too soon in the cycle. Also, make sure you always use the correct type of yeast – quick yeast specifically for bread machines.

- The flour may not have been suitable – it may not have been strong bread flour or there may have been too much low-gluten flour – such as rye or barley – in the mix.

The bread has a very open, bubbly, 'crumpet' texture

This may be caused by too much liquid or too much yeast. Alternatively, the salt may have been missed out.

Loose, completely unbaked flour is visible round the corners of the loaf

This can sometimes happen with more competitively priced machines. In future, check early on in the cycle and give things a helping hand with a flexible spatula. Also, check you have added the ingredients in the right order for your machine – usually liquid first.

The bread is too dry

This is most likely because there was not enough liquid. Some ingredients, typically wholemeal flour, can absorb extra liquid, so check that you added the correct amount. If you are sure you did, try adding an extra 10ml of liquid the next time you make the same bread. If it is still too dry add a further 10ml the next time.

The bread is too dense, soft, and the centre is still raw

This is likely to be caused by too much liquid and not enough flour. Check your machine's instruction book for typical flour to liquid ratios for your machine.

Dried fruit or other ingredients meant to stay whole have been incorporated into the mix

They have been added too early in the cycle: always use the **Raisin option**.

The loaf looks a bit wonky and lopsided, possibly with a bumpy, gnarled and knobbly top crust

This is likely to be caused by not quite enough liquid and too much flour.

The loaf may still be good to eat though, even if it does look a bit eccentric.

The loaf is risen but has a completely flat top, possibly blistered

It may be that the ratio of water to flour isn't ideal for your machine. Try decreasing the water slightly and/or increasing the amount of flour. Keep a note for next time.

What's that burning smell?

This can be alarming but is caused by ingredients – usually dried fruit – coming into contact with the heating element. In the unlikely event of the smell being an electrical burning smell, this is something quite different and altogether more serious. If this happens turn off the power at the socket immediately.

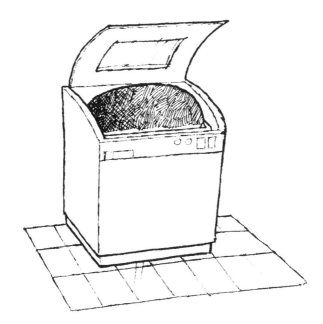

Index